ON LIBERALISM

The MIT Press's publishing mission benefits from the generosity of our donors, including Michael Dornbrook.

ON LIBERALISM

IN DEFENSE OF FREEDOM

CASS R. SUNSTEIN

The MIT Press
Cambridge, Massachusetts
London, England

The MIT Press
Massachusetts Institute of Technology
77 Massachusetts Avenue, Cambridge, MA 02139
mitpress.mit.edu

The MIT Press would like to thank the anonymous peer reviewers who provided comments on drafts of this book. The generous work of academic experts is essential for establishing the authority and quality of our publications. We acknowledge with gratitude the contributions of these otherwise uncredited readers.

This book was set in ITC Stone Serif Std and ITC Stone Sans Std by New Best-set Typesetters Ltd. Printed and bound in the United States of America.

Library of Congress Cataloging-in-Publication Data

Names: Sunstein, Cass R. author
Title: On liberalism / Cass R. Sunstein.
Description: Cambridge, Massachusetts : The MIT Press, [2025] | Includes
    bibliographical references and index.
Identifiers: LCCN 2024046957 (print) | LCCN 2024046958 (ebook) |
    ISBN 9780262049771 hardcover | ISBN 9780262383684 pdf |
    ISBN 9780262383691 epub
Subjects: LCSH: Liberalism—Philosophy | Liberalism—History | Hayek, Friedrich A.
    von (Friedrich August), 1899-1992 | Mill, John Stuart, 1806-1873
Classification: LCC JC574 .S86 2025 (print) | LCC JC574 (ebook) |
    DDC 320.5109—dc23/eng/20250328
LC record available at https://lccn.loc.gov/2024046957
LC ebook record available at https://lccn.loc.gov/2024046958

10 9 8 7 6 5 4 3 2 1

EU Authorised Representative: Easy Access System Europe, Mustamäe tee 50, 10621 Tallinn, Estonia | Email: gpsr.requests@easproject.com

Compulsory unification of opinion achieves only the unanimity of the graveyard.
—Robert Jackson

Whatever crushes individuality is despotism, by whatever name it may be called and whether it professes to be enforcing the will of God or the injunctions of men.
—John Stuart Mill

All life is an experiment. The more experiments in life you make, the better.
—Ralph Waldo Emerson

CONTENTS

PREFACE

Liberals prize two things above all: freedom and pluralism. Freedom is associated with agency. In liberal societies, people are allowed and encouraged to establish their own path, to take it if they like, and to reverse course if they want to do that. Liberals think that people should be allowed to be authors of the narratives of their own lives. Pluralism follows from the commitment to freedom. Some people will want to marry; some people will not want to marry. Some people will want to have children; some people will not want to have children. Because liberals believe in freedom and pluralism, many of them are romantics. They like it when people fall in love. They think that people should be allowed to have secrets, and to keep them to themselves.

Liberals promote freedom from fear. They want people to feel safe.

Who is not a liberal?

Adolf Hitler was not a liberal. Joseph Stalin was not a liberal. Vladimir Putin is not a liberal. If you do not believe in freedom of thought and freedom of speech, you are not a liberal. If you do not believe in freedom of religion, you are not a liberal. If you reject the idea of pluralism, you are not a liberal. If you do not believe in experiments in living, you are not a liberal (and I will have a fair bit to say on that topic). If you do not believe in the rule of law, you are not a liberal. Antiliberals and postliberals are not liberals (though they may share certain liberal convictions; we should certainly hope so).

George Orwell's *Nineteen Eighty-Four* is a shattering depiction of antiliberalism. One of Orwell's chief villains offers this warning: "If you want a

picture of the future, imagine a boot stamping on a human face—for ever."[1]
And consider this: "All this marching up and down and cheering and waving flags is simply sex gone sour."[2] Here are the novel's chilling last words:
"But it was all right, everything was all right, the struggle was finished. He
had won the victory over himself. He loved Big Brother."[3]

More than at any time since World War II, liberalism is under pressure,
even siege.[4] There is a lot of marching up and down. People are cheering.
Plenty of them are waving flags. Many of them seem to love Big Brother.
They hope that they have found him.

On the right, some people have given up on liberalism. They hold it
responsible for the collapse of the family and traditional values, rampant
criminality, disrespect for authority, and widespread immorality.

On the left, some people despise liberalism. They insist that it is old
and exhausted and dying. They think that it lacks the resources to handle
the problems posed by entrenched inequalities, racism, sexism, corporate
power, and environmental degradation. They refer to "neoliberalism" with
disdain. They do not respect the liberal political tradition.

Fascists reject liberalism. So do populists who think that freedom is over-
rated. In ways large and small, antiliberalism is on the march. So is tyranny.

Many of the marchers do not depict liberalism accurately; they offer a
caricature. They describe liberalism in a way that no liberal could possibly
endorse. They neglect the history of liberalism. They neglect philosophical
debates about liberalism, and within it. Perhaps more than ever, there is an
urgent need for a clear understanding of liberalism—of its core commitments, of its breadth, of its internal debates, of its evolving character, of its
promise, of what it is and what it can be.

What is a liberal? Who is a liberal? Any answer must start by saying
something about freedom. Liberals are committed to freedom of religion.
They believe in freedom of speech. They do not merely acknowledge pluralism and the freedom that makes it possible; they cherish these things.
They are committed to the rule of law. They welcome dissent. They believe
in experiments in living.

Among historians, it is standard to attempt to specify the origins of liberalism, and to focus on the particular role of French, German, and British thinkers in helping to create it.[5] We know that long before the rise of
liberalism, the word *liberal* referred to certain character traits: generosity
and openness of spirit, alongside a commitment to others, to the public

interest, and to the common good, rather than to one's own self-interest.[6] The accompanying noun was *liberality*, not *liberalism*.[7] During the Middle Ages, Christian values, including charity, were connected with liberality.[8] The term *liberal* was associated with concern for the common good, rather than opposition to it, and was not connected with a focus (solely) on one's self-interest.

In 1628, John Donne said that "Christ is a liberal God." He urged that people should find "new ways to be liberal."[9] In his "city upon a hill" sermon in 1630, John Winthrop argued that the difficult times required "extraordinary liberality," in which the colonists would "bear one another's burdens."[10] The idea of "liberality" entailed a willingness to help to reduce the suffering of others. Similarly, John Locke, sometimes counted as the first liberal philosopher, contended that children ought to learn to be "kind, liberal and civil."[11] Once more, Locke's use of the word *liberal* was closely connected with liberality.

During the seventeenth and eighteenth centuries, people did not speak of *liberalism*.[12] In 1772, the *Oxford English Dictionary* drew on long-standing understandings in saying that the word "liberal" meant "free from bias, prejudice, or bigotry; open-minded, tolerant."[13] Importantly and revealingly, liberality became closely associated with the idea of religious toleration, which was a particularly central concern during the late eighteenth century.[14] It remains a central concern today.

In 1790, George Washington wrote, "As mankind become more liberal they will be more apt to allow that all those who conduct themselves as worthy members of the community are equally entitled to the protection of civil government."[15] Here Washington offered a strong signal of the importance of respect for pluralism, which has of course become central to the liberal tradition. Washington also associated the idea of being "more liberal" with a conception of equal protection of the law, which became part of the United States Constitution after the Civil War. The adjective *liberal* was widely applied to that Constitution after its ratification in 1789, even though the word *liberalism* was not in use.[16]

The idea of liberalism, as such, arose in France in the early nineteenth century, probably around 1811.[17] It did so in the aftermath of the French Revolution, when people sought to defend the basic principles for which that revolution had been fought, with a particular emphasis on (1) the rule of law, (2) representative government, (3) freedom of the press, and (4) freedom of religion. Benjamin Constant and Madame de Staël were defining figures here.[18] It is important to emphasize that in its origins, liberalism was not at all associated with a focus on greed and self-interest. On the contrary, it owed a great deal to previous understandings of what it meant to be liberal. Madame de Staël wrote, "What we need is a lever against egoism."[19] No early liberal argued that human beings were asocial creatures, unmoored from social bonds, the family, culture, religion, and tradition.

In 1815, Constant wrote a defining book with a stunningly ambitious title: *Principles of Politics Applicable to All Governments*. The book called for popular sovereignty and hence a form of democracy, and also for a set of freedoms, including freedom of thought, freedom of the press, and freedom of religion. Constant insisted on the importance of the separation of church and state. One of his central themes was the need to ensure that the state, and the law, would respect pluralism with respect to belief and action. Drawing on older traditions, Constant also emphasized the importance of self-sacrifice, virtue, generosity, and dedication to the common good.[20] Wilhelm Traugott Krug, a Prussian philosopher, published his *Historical Depiction of Liberalism* in 1823; this was probably the first attempt at a history of liberalism (and it was pretty early indeed).[21] In the next decades, the modern idea of liberalism was essentially born.

Since that time, liberalism has been subject to an extraordinary number of twists and turns. In some times and places, liberalism has been closely identified with respect for free markets, free trade, and private property (*classical liberalism* or *neoliberalism*; see chapter 6). In some times and places, liberalism has been identified with a government determined to provide social services and help those at the bottom of the economic ladder (*New Deal liberalism*; see chapter 7). Many social democrats are liberal. Some liberals emphasize *negative rights*: rights to be free from coercion and intrusion, above all from government. Other liberals emphasize *positive rights*: rights to receive government help, such as education, housing, and health care (again see chapter 7). Liberals who emphasize such rights do not favor government control of the economy; they believe in free markets. But they want to help those at the bottom, and to give everyone a fair chance (see chapter 8).

In some times and places, liberalism has leaned technocratic, with an emphasis on the importance of experts and expertise. In some times and places, liberalism has leaned populist, with an emphasis on the need for accountability and public control. While rights of some kind have always been a part of liberalism, the strong emphasis on freedom of choice and individual rights, as liberalism's foundation or core, is relatively recent. Still, that emphasis has continuity with the work of the early liberal theorists, who emphasized freedom of conscience, speech, and religion, and who sought to make space for pluralism.

In political philosophy, it is standard to emphasize the liberal commitment to freedom, but also to make a distinction between two kinds of liberalism. Some people, like John Rawls and Charles Larmore, endorse what they call *political liberalism*.[22] They think that different people, from radically different starting points, ought to be able to accept certain liberal principles. Political liberals think that Christians, Jews, Muslims, Hindus, agnostics, and atheists can embrace the basic liberties. They believe that those with different philosophical commitments can agree to be liberals. Rawls himself gives priority to this principle: "each person is to have an equal right to the most extensive basic liberty compatible with a similar liberty for others."[23] By way of elaboration, Rawls singles out the "basic liberties of citizens," which include "political liberty (the right to vote and to be eligible for public office) together with freedom of speech and assembly; liberty of conscience and freedom of thought; freedom of the person along with the right to hold (personal) property; and freedom from arbitrary arrest and seizure as defined by the concept of the rule of law."[24] We can understand this catalog as an effort to summarize the arc of liberal thought since the early nineteenth century.

Rawls refers to a liberal idea about legitimacy: "Our exercise of political power is fully proper only when it is exercised in accordance with a constitution the essentials of which all citizens as free and equal may reasonably be expected to endorse in the light of principles and ideals acceptable to their common human reason."[25] Note here the emphasis on human agency. All citizens are taken to be "free and equal," and they are put in the driver's seat, equipped with their "common human reason." Rawls urges that liberal principles can be endorsed by people with different "comprehensive doctrines"—that is, doctrines about right and wrong, good and evil, the existence of God, and the foundations of morality and politics.[26]

By contrast, some people, like John Stuart Mill, Immanuel Kant, and Joseph Raz, are *perfectionist liberals*. They think that liberalism is not only a doctrine about political legitimacy. In their view, liberalism offers an account of what it means to have a good life. They believe that liberalism should be founded on a commitment to individual autonomy, in which each of us is allowed to be the author of the narrative of our own lives. Those who do not give pride of place to individual autonomy will not be enthusiastic about perfectionist liberalism, though they should be open to political liberalism. If you emphasize duty and faith, for example, the idea of autonomy might not be so central.

Political liberals object that perfectionist liberalism is too sectarian and hence illegitimate; it excludes people who would not make individual autonomy so central. For their part, perfectionist liberals believe that political liberalism gives up on liberalism's deepest moral foundations. Still, it is essential to see that both endorse the basic liberties.

Liberal philosophers disagree with one another about many other things as well. Some liberals, like Robert Nozick, are *libertarians*; they believe that redistribution from rich to poor is fundamentally unjust. Other liberals, like Rawls, do not share that belief at all. They might even believe that large-scale redistribution is mandatory. So long as you are committed to freedom, you can be a liberal whether you agree with Nozick or instead Rawls. Other liberals, like Philip Pettit, emphasize the central importance of a principle of freedom as *nondomination*, by which no one is subject to the will of another.

Whether we look to history or to philosophy, which form of liberalism is best? Of course I have my views, and they will make an appearance here. Above all, I will be emphasizing the idea of *experiments of living*, a term from John Stuart Mill with powerful implications for liberalism today. I will stress the importance of such experiments for both individual and social development, and the relationship between experiments in living and respect for individual agency. (Also: Three cheers for Rawls, and another three for Franklin Delano Roosevelt.) My larger goal is to offer a kind of portrait of liberalism now—of its big tent and its edges, of what it stands for, of what it stands against. Liberalism is indeed a big tent, but it is also a fighting faith.

I should emphasize that while there is some engagement with political philosophy here, this is not a work of political philosophy. My hope is that we can make a great deal of progress in understanding liberalism, and what is right with it, without answering the hardest theoretical questions.

This book is structured as follows. Chapter 1, the heart of the book, is a kind of manifesto, in the form of a long list of propositions, or sets of propositions, about liberalism. Chapter 2 explores the central idea of experiments of living, with a suggestion that a liberal constitutional order might give pride of place to that idea. As we shall see, the commitment to experiments of living helps to unify many liberal ideas. Chapter 3 turns to Mill and Friedrich Hayek, two of liberalism's greatest thinkers (and they haunt these pages), with an emphasis on what I see as the intensely personal sources of Mill's enthusiasm for experiments in living. For all his greatness, Hayek was insufficiently attuned to what made Mill tick, and to what (in my view) makes the best forms of liberalism tick. I love Hayek, but I love Mill more.

Chapter 4 gives an account of the rule of law as liberals understand it. As we shall see, the rule of law is a critical ideal, but a limited one. It should not be confused with other ideals and values. Chapter 5 explores freedom of speech, with specific reference to the question whether that form of freedom includes lies and falsehoods. I approach that question by explaining why liberals generally protect the thought they hate, including statements that are untrue.

Chapter 6 explores free markets and how liberals think about them. It explains how liberals think about regulation and when it is justified. It explores the relationship between classical liberalism and behavioral economics. (Disclosure: We're going to get a bit technical there.) Chapter 7 discusses, and largely embraces, Franklin Delano Roosevelt's Second Bill of Rights, which includes social and economic guarantees; it investigates where the Second Bill fits within the liberal tradition. Chapter 8 explores opportunity (from an admittedly unusual angle; you'll see). The epilogue offers some words about fire and hope.

1 ON BEING A LIBERAL

1. Liberals believe in six things: freedom, human rights, pluralism, security, the rule of law, and democracy. In fact, they believe in *deliberative democracy*, an approach that combines a commitment to reason-giving in the public sphere with a commitment to accountability.[1]

2. *Liberal authoritarianism* is an oxymoron. Because liberals believe in freedom, personal security, and pluralism, they reject authoritarianism in all its forms. Illiberal democracy is illiberal, and liberals oppose it for that reason.

3. Liberals are keenly aware that reasonable people disagree on many things, including the nature of a good life and which God to worship (if any). They seek to make space for these disagreements.

4. Liberals do not merely acknowledge pluralism; they cherish it, on the ground that it increases the likelihood that people will learn from one another and from experiments in living. Liberals want people who disagree with each other to find a way to live together, and to smile—or at least to nod respectfully—at their differences. They embrace these words from John Stuart Mill: "He who knows only his own side of the case knows little of that. His reasons may be good, and no one may have been able to refute them. But if he is equally unable to refute the reasons on the opposite side, if he does not so much as know what they are, he has no ground for preferring either opinion."[2]

5. The liberal emphasis on pluralism is closely connected to the liberal commitments to freedom and security. Those who reject pluralism render people unfree and insecure (and sometimes imprison or kill them).

6. Understood in this way, liberalism consists of a set of commitments in political theory and political philosophy, with significant implications for politics and law. In North America, Europe, and elsewhere, those who consider themselves to be "conservatives" may or may not embrace liberal commitments. Those who consider themselves to be "leftists" may or may not qualify as liberals. You can be, at once, a liberal, as understood here, and a conservative; you can be a leftist and illiberal. There are illiberal conservatives and illiberal leftists. In politics, James Madison, Alexander Hamilton, Franklin Delano Roosevelt, Winston Churchill, John F. Kennedy, Lyndon Johnson, Ronald Reagan, Margaret Thatcher, and Angela Merkel all count as part of the liberal tradition. This is so even though there are many fierce disagreements among them.

7. Abraham Lincoln was a liberal. Here is what he said in 1854: "If the negro *is* a man, is it not to that extent, a total destruction of self-government, to say that he too shall not govern *himself*? When the white man governs himself that is self-government; but when he governs himself, and also governs *another* man, that is *more* than self-government—that is despotism. . . . No man is good enough to govern another man, *without that other's consent*. I say this is the leading principle—the sheet anchor of American republicanism."[3]

We might change the term *American republicanism* to *liberalism*. The idea of a sheet anchor is a useful way of linking self-government, in people's individual capacities, with self-governance as a political ideal. A sheet anchor is not an ordinary anchor. It is the most reliable one you have, the one least likely to fail under extreme stress. It is the equivalent of a port in a storm. Liberals especially like this: "No man is good enough to govern another man, without that other's consent." They can embrace that general proposition while having disparate views about the right attitude toward long-standing traditions or the proper approach to smoking, abortion, immigration, alcohol consumption, artificial intelligence, climate change, and constitutional law.

8. We should connect Lincoln's sheet anchor to the animating liberal ideals: freedom, human rights, pluralism, security, the rule of law, and democracy.

9. While liberals have not always been committed to democracy, they have always been committed to freedom. Some liberals have thought that there is a right to immunity from the power of the state while also denying that

there is a right to self-governance, in the form of popular control of the power of the state. But Lincoln had it right. He captured the underlying logic of liberalism in linking freedom ("no man is good enough to govern another man, without that other's consent") with self-government and hence democracy. Freedom in one's personal life (a right to self-governance, writ small) is connected with freedom in one's civic life (a right to self-governance, writ large).

10. Liberals are committed to individual dignity. They see people as subjects rather than objects, and they prize the idea of *agency*. They agree with Lincoln: "If slavery is not wrong, nothing is wrong."[4] For that reason, they regard Mill's great work *The Subjection of Women* as helping to define the essence of liberalism.[5] Thus Mill wrote, "The legal subordination of one sex to the other—is wrong in itself and now one of the chief hindrances to human improvement."[6]

11. Liberals note that Mill's argument is an extended version of Lincoln's remarks on slavery. With Mill and Lincoln, they insist on a link between their commitment to liberty and a particular conception of equality, which can be seen as a kind of *anticaste principle*. If some people are subjected to the will of others, we have a violation of liberal ideals.[7] Many liberals have invoked an anticaste principle to combat entrenched forms of inequality based on race, sex, and disability. They insist that in many nations, those forms of inequality have involved, or now involve, the imposition of something like a caste system.

12. Liberals oppose censorship. They are committed to free and fair elections and hence the right to vote. They work to defend freedom of conscience, the right of privacy, economic opportunity, and the right to be different. They agree with Oliver Wendell Holmes Jr., who embraced "the principle of free thought—not free thought for those who agree with us but freedom for the thought that we hate."[8]

13. Liberals are aware that all over the globe, liberalism is under siege. They see Hitler, Mussolini, Stalin, and Mao as defining practitioners of antiliberalism. Hitler said that one of his chief goals was "to abolish the liberal concept of the individual."[9] Mussolini proclaimed that fascism was "the negation of liberalism."[10] Liberals see Karl Marx and German political theorist (and Nazi party member) Carl Schmitt as defining antiliberal theorists. They regard Vladimir Putin and Viktor Orban as contemporary antiliberals.

They know that prominent antiliberal leaders, of various kinds, are easy to find in the United States and Europe.

14. Liberals believe that freedom of speech is an essential way of making self-government real. They understand freedom of speech to encompass not only political speech, but also literature, music, and the arts in general (including cinema). In fact, they insist on that point. They think that the arts broaden the imagination, including the political imagination. Liberals admire John Milton, William Blake, Jane Austen, and James Joyce. They also admire Walt Whitman ("I am as bad as the worst, but, thank God, I am as good as the best") and Bob Dylan ("Even the president of the United States sometimes must have to stand naked").

15. Liberals much like Justice Robert Jackson's words: "Compulsory unification of opinion achieves only the unanimity of the graveyard."[11] Liberals who insist on that proposition do not claim that people must declare their fidelity to liberal principles, including that one. They also like this from Justice Jackson: "Those who begin coercive elimination of dissent soon find themselves exterminating dissenters."[12] Liberals have diverse views about social media, but they do not favor censorship of social media platforms.

16. Freedom of religion is fundamental to liberalism.[13] Indeed, many of liberalism's deepest convictions grew out of an insistence on religious liberty. Consistent with their commitment to pluralism, liberals believe that people should be allowed to worship in their own way, or not to worship at all. In North America and Europe in particular, many Christians believe that their liberalism is a product of their faith. Other religious traditions, including Judaism, Hinduism, Islam, and Buddhism, include countless liberals. As a matter of history, Catholicism and liberalism have sometimes been at odds, but properly understood, liberalism and Catholicism are highly compatible; Catholicism has helped to define contemporary liberalism, and many Catholics have been great liberals. David Tracy of the University of Chicago is a contemporary example.

17. Countless liberals have deep religious convictions. They are acutely aware that all over the world, some people of faith abhor the idea of separating church and state and insist that the government should embrace and even enforce certain religious commitments. But liberals want to make the state free from domination by any religion, and they seek to ensure that the state guarantees safety for every religion.

18. Liberals think that any intrusion on the freedom of religious believers should be presumed to be unacceptable, though of course no one is allowed to commit acts of violence (murder, rape, assault). Liberals think that officials should not be allowed to forbid people from worshipping in their own way. They also believe in the separation of church and state, even as they recognize that reasonable people disagree about what that separation entails. Liberals can and do disagree about specific issues involving religious liberty, including the scope of the Establishment Clause in the United States Constitution. In the United States, Supreme Court Justice Neil Gorsuch is a liberal; so is Justice Elena Kagan.

19. If postliberals or antiliberalists insist on an official religious orthodoxy, liberals will respond: Who do you think you are?

20. The idea of the rule of law is central to liberalism. It is closely connected with Lincoln's sheet anchor. As liberals understand it, the idea entails a commitment to seven principles: (1) clear, general, publicly accessible rules laid down in advance; (2) law that is prospective, allowing people to plan, rather than retroactive, defeating people's expectations; (3) conformity between law on the books and law in the world; (4) rights to a hearing ("due process of law"); (5) some degree of separation between those who make the law and those who interpret the law; (6) no unduly rapid changes in the law; and (7) no contradictions or palpable inconsistency in the law.[14] The rule of law is not the same as a commitment to freedom of speech, freedom of religion, or freedom from unreasonable searches and seizures. It is a distinctive ideal, and liberals embrace it as such. (I take this issue up in more detail in chapter 4.)

21. Liberals prize free markets, on the ground that they provide an important means by which people exercise their agency (see chapter 6). In addition, liberals never forget that free markets promote economic growth. Liberals believe that economic growth is important for a wide range of important things, above all well-being, including or perhaps especially for those at the bottom of the economic ladder.

22. Liberals abhor monopolies, public or private, on the ground that they are highly likely to compromise freedom. Consider consumers: free markets allow them to buy what they want. (Let us bracket the question of wealth; poor people cannot, of course, buy what they want.) Consider workers, who can choose among the available options; liberals are committed to the

idea of "careers open to talents" (see chapter 8). Consider employers, who can hire whom they wish (with important qualifications, as in the prohibition on race and sex discrimination).[15]

23. At the same time, liberals know that markets can fail, as, for example, when workers or consumers lack information, or when consumption of energy produces environmental harm. Liberals believe that a range of tools are available to combat market failure. They might favor provision of information to consumers. They might favor corrective taxes or regulation to address environmental harm (see chapter 6).

24. Liberals firmly believe in the right to private property. They think that on grounds of autonomy and welfare, that right is exceedingly important. The right to private property increases security and personal independence. It promotes freedom from fear. It increases political independence; if your property is yours, you have a degree of immunity from the state. It is also associated with economic growth.

25. At the same time, nothing in liberalism forbids a progressive income tax, or is inconsistent with large-scale redistribution from rich to poor. Liberals can disagree about the progressive income tax or on whether and when redistribution is a good idea.[16] Some liberals admire Lyndon Johnson's Great Society; some liberals do not.

26. Many liberals are drawn to John Stuart Mill's harm principle: "The only purpose for which power can be rightfully exercised over any member of a civilized community, against his will, is to prevent harm to others."[17] Liberals prize what Mill called *experiments of living*, and they are alert to the potentially harmful effects of both coercion and conformity.[18] (Much more on that in chapter 2.) Liberals know that different people reasonably seek different paths, and they believe that there are many ways of having a good life. Liberals think that people should have access to both marriage and divorce.[19]

27. Some liberals ultimately reject the harm principle, and even if they tend to like it, they do not take it as a dogma, or as rigid and fixed. Liberals are also aware that the harm principle can be challenging to define.[20] It is fully consistent with the liberal tradition to emphasize that people might lack relevant information or make terrible mistakes.[21] Many liberals like laws that require people to wear seat belts; many liberals do not. Many

liberals are enthusiastic about the contemporary administrative state; many liberals are not.[22]

28. Many liberals are generally receptive to *nudges*, understood as freedom-preserving interventions such as warnings, reminders, and disclosure of information.[23] But some liberals worry that nudges can turn into shoves, or that they might not be sufficiently respectful of the autonomy of those who are nudged (see chapter 6).

29. Many liberals are Kantians; they insist that people should be treated as ends, not means.[24] They are liberals *because* they are Kantians. They think that liberalism is compelled by, or is part and parcel of, their Kantianism.

30. Many liberals are utilitarians, seeking to maximize social welfare; they are liberals *because* they are utilitarians. They think that liberalism is likely to increase social welfare. In particular, they think that freedom increases welfare. They say this even though liberals do not agree on how to specify the broad idea of "welfare." They know that some people, like Jeremy Bentham, emphasize "happiness," and seek to maximize pleasure and minimize pain. They know that other liberals, like Mill, emphasize that human beings care about many things, and that "welfare" might include, for example, a sense of meaning or purpose, even if it does not bring about "happiness." They know that some liberals are romantics and emphasize self-development (see chapter 3).

31. Many liberals, known as *contractarians*, find it useful to emphasize the idea of a "social contract" between free and equal persons; they are liberals *because* they are contractarians. They think that free and equal persons would agree to liberal principles (see chapter 5). Some liberals observe that Kantianism, utilitarianism, and contractarianism tend to converge.[25] They are delighted to make that observation.

32. Many people believe that their religious tradition compels, or is compatible with, liberalism. Far from seeing a conflict between liberalism and their faith, they think that their faith leads directly to, or fits well with, their liberalism. (Liberals do not mind a little repetition.)

33. Liberals can take their own side in a quarrel.[26]

34. Liberals like laughter. They are anti-anti-laughter.

35. Although liberals like liberalism, they do not like tribalism. They are concerned when people sort themselves into different groups, defined in

specific ways, and see other people as part of other groups, defined in other ways. Liberals tend to think that tribalism is an obstacle to mutual respect and even to productive interactions. They are intensely uncomfortable with discussions that start "I am an X and you are a Y," and that proceed accordingly. Skeptical of "identity politics," liberals think that each of us has many different identities, and that it is usually best to focus on the merits of issues, not on one or another "identity."

36. Liberals know that people who have different life experiences (including, for example, the experience of discrimination, marginalization, or oppression) will know important things by virtue of those experiences. In fact, they insist on that point. But to liberals, a constant or excessive emphasis on a single aspect of "identity" tends to separate and calcify people and to endanger productive discussions, whether we are speaking of crime, poverty, education, climate change, or democracy itself.

37. Liberals are aware that if identity politics are taken to an extreme, they threaten to produce horrors. Liberals know that these issues are exceedingly complicated.

38. Liberals hope that people with diverse backgrounds and views can embrace liberalism, or at least certain forms of liberalism. Many liberals enthusiastically support John Rawls's idea of an *overlapping consensus*, in which people accept the broad principles of what Rawls calls *political liberalism*. Political liberalism is meant to accommodate people with different views about fundamental matters, including different religious views. It can easily be supported by people on the left, on the right, and in the center.[27]

39. Many liberals also embrace the idea of *incompletely theorized agreements*, by which people who are uncertain about fundamental matters, or who disagree about fundamental matters, can agree about certain practices or principles, such as protection of the right to dissent and religious liberty.[28] You can believe in freedom of speech because you are a Kantian, insisting that people should be treated as ends, not means. You can believe in freedom of speech because you are a utilitarian, seeking to increase social utility. You can believe in freedom of speech because you are a romantic.

40. Because liberals do not like tribalism, many of them do not especially love writing about why they are liberals, opposed to illiberals, postliberals, and antiliberals. It might even pain them to do so. They do not like

thinking of liberalism as any kind of tribe. Still, they disagree with illiberals, postliberals, and antiliberals. They regret that some illiberals, postliberals, and antiliberals seem not to understand what liberalism actually is, or characterize it in ways that render it unrecognizable.[29] They also regret that some illiberals, postliberals, and antiliberals do know what liberalism actually is, and that they are unwilling to respect freedom, democracy, the rule of law, and reasonable pluralism.

41. Liberals think that some purported antiliberals are charlatans or snake oil salesmen. They think that some antiliberals have manufactured an opponent and called it *liberalism*, without sufficiently engaging with the liberal tradition, in all its diversity, or with actual liberal thinkers. They agree with Amos Tversky and Daniel Kahneman: "The refutation of a caricature can be no more than a caricature of refutation."[30] They think that some antiliberals wrongly conflate liberalism with something bad or terrible that happened last year or last week, or with enthusiasm for greed, for the pursuit of self-interest, and for rejection of norms of self-restraint. Far from being charitable to those they deem to be their opponents, they describe liberalism in a way that no liberal could endorse or even recognize.

42. Liberals suspect that some antiliberals, on the right and left, greatly enjoy being part of a large-scale movement, and like seeing themselves as part of a vanguard or as revolutionaries, without having or offering clarity or details on what their movement is for or against, or on what their movement would achieve, if it were successful.

43. Liberals agree that some of those on the left and the right who claim to be postliberals, or antiliberals, have legitimate claims and concerns about matters of great importance (including crime, corruption, immorality, a lack of educational opportunity, and poverty), and that they point to real and serious problems in existing societies. They do not think that liberal societies are close to perfect. But they do not think that those legitimate claims and concerns should count as objections to liberalism as such. (More on this in chapter 4.)

44. Liberals are keenly aware that some critics of liberalism, following Tocqueville, insist that certain kinds of attitudes, institutions, norms, and virtues are essential, and that liberalism cannot work or survive without them. Many liberals share that belief. Some people believe that human beings are

spiritual by nature, and that if religious faith atrophies, liberal societies will crumble. Some people believe that civic virtue is essential and that liberalism needs it. Some people emphasize the importance of the nuclear family, and urge that without it, liberal societies will fall apart. Many liberals share these beliefs.

45. Many liberals will also say: We are liberals. We have something to say about freedom, human rights, pluralism, the rule of law, security, and democracy. *We do not have something to say about everything.* As liberals, we have nothing to say about many things. We are interested in what other people say about things of great importance. We will learn from those things. We know that liberal societies may depend on things on which liberalism, as such, is silent. It is not liberalism's job to supply those things.

46. Liberalism is a wide tent.[31] John Locke thought differently from Adam Smith, and Rawls fundamentally disagreed with Mill.[32] Here are some liberals: Immanuel Kant, Benjamin Constant, Adam Smith, Jeremy Bentham, Mary Wollstonecraft, John Dewey, Friedrich Hayek, John Maynard Keynes, Isaiah Berlin, Jurgen Habermas, Joseph Raz, Edna Ullmann-Margalit, Amartya Sen, Jeremy Waldron, Milton Friedman, Ronald Dworkin, Robert Nozick, Susan Okin, Charles Larmore, Christine Korsgaard, Phillip Pettit, Alan Ryan, B. Douglas Bernheim, and Martha Nussbaum. These people differ on fundamental matters. Some liberals, like Hayek and Friedman, emphasize the problems with centralized planning; other liberals, like Rawls and Raz, are not focused on that question at all. Some liberals, like Mill, Wollstonecraft, Nussbaum, Ullmann-Margalit, Sen, and Okin, focus directly on sex equality; other liberals, like Kant and Smith, do not have much to say about that topic.

47. Liberals argue fiercely with one another. Rawls and Nozick differ on fundamental matters; Nozick was a critic of Rawls. Larmore and Raz are in sharp disagreement. Hayek and Keynes were not in accord.

48. Many of the important *practitioners* of liberalism—from James Madison and Alexander Hamilton to Abraham Lincoln to Franklin Delano Roosevelt to Martin Luther King Jr. to Margaret Thatcher and Ronald Reagan—did not commit themselves to foundational philosophical commitments of any kind (such as Kantianism or utilitarianism). This is so even if some of them were, in an important sense, political thinkers.

49. It is possible to be a liberal and to agree with Hayek and thus to insist on the evils of socialism and the importance of free markets (see chapters 5 and 8).[33] It is possible to be a liberal and to agree with Rawls and thus to be open to (some forms of what is sometimes called) socialism and to downplay the centrality of free markets.[34] A liberal might think that Ronald Reagan was a great president and that Franklin Delano Roosevelt was an abomination; a liberal might think that Franklin Delano Roosevelt was a great president and that Ronald Reagan was an abomination.

50. Liberals have divergent views about *negative liberty* (understood as freedom from coercion) and *positive liberty* (understood to include rights to certain goods, such as food and housing), and about whether there is a meaningful difference between them. Some liberals insist that properly understood, freedom entails a right not to be intruded on, above all by government. For them, freedom does not include a right to housing, education, employment, or subsistence. Some liberals answer that negative liberty requires a positive government, willing and able to protect people's security. In their view, all rights are positive rights. Some liberals believe that nations should recognize rights to housing, education, welfare, and subsistence. (For more on this, see chapter 7.)

51. Liberals value the size of their tent, even as they disagree sharply with one another. Most liberals dislike it (a lot) when someone claims that one form of liberalism is liberal and that others are not. Most liberals like it when Hayekians or Millians, fiercely devoted to their form of liberalism, agree that many liberals are not Hayekians and have serious reservations about Mill. Most liberals do not like it at all when some ill-tempered liberals (enthusiastic, say, about free markets) object that other liberals (in favor of, say, New Deal liberalism or social democracy) are not really liberals. Still, they are aware that it is important and even crucial to choose the right form of liberalism.

52. Many political conservatives are liberals. Milton Friedman and Thomas Sowell, often described as free market conservatives, are liberals. Because of his attack on rationalism, Michael Oakeshott, a celebrated conservative, is probably not best characterized as a liberal (though liberals tend to respect him and to find him intriguing). On this count, Edmund Burke, an eloquent defender of traditions, is not simple to characterize (and liberals disagree about whether to claim him as one of their own; see chapter 4).

53. Many leftists are liberals, but Marxists are not liberals, and leftists who reject freedom of speech, and who do not respect religious liberty or the rule of law, are to that extent illiberal. Consider Morton Horwitz's illiberal words:[35]

> I do not see how a Man of the Left can describe the rule of law as "an unqualified human good"! It undoubtedly restrains power, but it also prevents power's benevolent exercise. It creates formal equality—a not inconsiderable virtue—but it promotes substantive inequality by creating a consciousness that radically separates law from politics, means from ends, processes from outcomes. By promoting procedural justice it enables the shrewd, the calculating, and the wealthy to manipulate its forms to their own advantage. And it ratifies and legitimates an adversarial, competitive, and atomistic conception of human relations.

Liberals do not agree with any of this.

54. Liberals do not believe that liberalism is a "thing." They do not think that you can go in a time machine, seek out Constant, Mill, Hayek, Rawls, Habermas, Nussbaum, Pettit, or Raz, and claim that you have found liberalism. Keenly aware that liberals disagree with one another, they insist that debates over the right understanding of liberalism are *interpretive* in Ronald Dworkin's sense.[36] Dworkin urges that when people engage in interpretation, they must "fit" what they are interpreting. They cannot say that Shakespeare's Hamlet is really about skydiving, or that the U.S. Constitution forbids people to walk. At the same time, Dworkin adds, some objects of interpretation can be understood in more than one way. If we have a choice, we should interpret texts in a way that makes them the best they can be—in a way that makes them appealing rather than the opposite. With respect to liberalism, Rawls did that, and so did Raz, and so does Pettit, and so does Habermas.

55. Those who defend their own understanding of liberalism must "fit" the defining principles; they cannot reject the idea of freedom, or deplore Lincoln's sheet anchor, or reject the rule of law. But those principles can be understood in different ways. It follows that liberals defending their own understanding also seek to "justify" liberalism, in the sense that they attempt to put it in the best constructive light, or to make it as worthy of support as it can possibly be. A liberal who believes in the right to choose abortion would have to argue that freedom, rightly understood, includes that right. A liberal who does not believe in the right to choose abortion would make the opposite argument. Liberals disagree about whether the

right to free speech includes the right to write and read pornography. A Rawlsian liberal should agree that a Hayekian liberal is a liberal (and welcome Hayekians as such), but would claim that Rawlsian liberalism is superior, in principle, to Hayekian liberalism.

56. Internal disagreements among liberals sometimes operate along the axis of *fit*; more commonly, they operate along the axis of *justification*. Sometimes internal debates among liberals purport to involve fit, but they actually involve justification. People are trying to figure out the best version, or specification, of liberalism. Liberals who disagree about that matter might be glad to emphasize that these are arguments among people who are in fundamental agreement about many matters.

57. It is possible for a society to be liberal in some respects but illiberal in other respects. Before the Civil War, the United States was liberal in many ways, but it allowed slavery (and a system of racial caste long after abolition). The United Kingdom has long been deeply committed to liberal principles, but until relatively recently, it engaged in, promoted, or permitted rampant sex discrimination. People who think that they are postliberal or antiliberal might be liberal in important respects, at least in the sense that they agree with liberals on fundamental matters. Some contemporary nations are liberal in important ways but illiberal in other ways.

58. Liberalism is a work in progress. Liberals are not sad about that.

59. Liberals may or may not agree with "the left"; they may or may not agree with "the right."[37] They may or may not embrace "libertarianism," which prizes freedom of contract and opposes the modern regulatory state. Libertarians emphasize the free market; they might well disapprove of minimum wage legislation, maximum hour legislation, and prohibitions on employment discrimination. All libertarians are liberals, but most liberals are not libertarians; they do not regard freedom of contract as sacrosanct, and they are fine with minimum wage legislation, maximum hour legislation, and prohibitions on employment discrimination.

60. Liberals think that those on the left are illiberal if they are not (for example) committed to freedom of speech and viewpoint diversity. They do not like idea of orthodoxy, including on university campuses.

61. Liberals favor, and recognize the need for, a robust civil society, including a wide range of private associations (some of which reject liberalism).

They believe in the importance of social norms, including norms of civility, considerateness, charity, and self-restraint. They do not want to censor any antiliberals or postliberals, even though some antiliberals or postliberals would not return the favor. On this count, they turn the other cheek. They note that people on the right might be more liberal than people on the left. Whether this is so depends on which people we are talking about, and when we are talking about them.

62. Liberals have antiliberal, illiberal, and postliberal friends. Liberals like having friends. They like having friends with disparate views.

63. Many liberals are greatly puzzled by some of those who favor "postliberalism." They know that nations that are liberal in important respects are illiberal in other respects, and that for one or another reason, nations that are liberal in important respects face serious challenges. Still, they are puzzled because they are not sure what it is that postliberals are "post."

64. Liberals notice that some "postliberals," especially on the right, identify liberalism with something that almost all liberals reject—a commitment to pleasure-seeking and sexual hedonism, and a rejection of self-control and norms of civility and considerateness. Liberalism should not be identified with the Playboy philosophy (held by Hugh Hefner, the founder of that magazine).

65. Liberals do not regard the many failures of existing nations that are often defined as liberal—including (for example) the United States, the United Kingdom, Canada, Ireland, Denmark, Germany, the Netherlands, Sweden, Finland, and France—as reflections of the failures of liberalism.[38] Nor are the failures, in the main, best characterized as "a failure to live up to liberal ideals" (though some of them are). They are failures of other kinds, mostly involving policy and practice. They are not failures of a theory, or of political thinkers such as Mill or Rawls.

66. If the objection is that free markets have serious limits, and that a great deal of regulation might be justified on grounds of efficiency, redistribution, or fairness, liberals are likely to say: very possibly so (see chapter 6).

67. If the claim is that "neoliberalism" is a bad idea, liberals are likely to say: We are not sure what *neoliberalism* is, because the term is mostly used by people who hate it. But if it is identified with deregulation and an insistence on the ceaseless wonders of free markets, then liberals need not, and

many liberals do not, embrace neoliberalism. Liberals like free markets, but they do not believe that they are sacrosanct. They have an account of "market failure," and it is not frozen in time (see chapter 6). Although liberals argue with one another about what counts as a market failure, most of them want to regulate monopolies and to control externalities (harms imposed on third parties, as in the case of pollution). Many of them also want to control *internalities*, which arise when people impose harm on their future selves (consider cigarette taxes and alcohol taxes, or laws requiring seat belt bucking). Liberals are not enthusiastic about government paternalism, but most of them do not rule it out of bounds (see again chapter 6).

68. If the objection is to certain claims for sexual liberty, liberals are likely to ask: What do you have in mind? Liberals believe in freedom of choice, but they do not believe in sexual assault, domestic violence, or child abuse. Liberals are highly likely to oppose criminal restrictions on same-sex behavior, but they will not want to require people to speak or act in ways that violate their religious convictions. Liberals are nowadays likely to accept same-sex marriage and to ask those who do oppose same-sex marriage to explain their opposition (without resorting to question-begging claims about what marriage is).

69. Liberals are especially puzzled by certain claims about what they themselves seek, or what they themselves are against. Recall that many liberals embrace *political liberalism* (understood as a philosophical position), which takes no stand on (many) conceptions of what is right and what is good, and which makes plenty of space for people with divergent values, including for those who reject Mill's version of liberalism (which puts a high premium on individual autonomy).

70. People can think, act, and worship in different ways. Jews, Christians, Muslims, Hindus, Buddhists, atheists, agnostics: liberals welcome each and all.

71. If the claim of postliberals or antiliberals is that liberalism itself consists of an official orthodoxy, liberals will respond: not guilty. Liberalism is not an official orthodoxy in the same sense that Nazism was, or that a state committed to a particular religion would be. Liberalism makes room for a host of unofficial orthodoxies. Liberals embrace a principle of toleration or (better—much better) mutual respect. You can call that an official orthodoxy if you like, but you really shouldn't.

72. It is true, of course, that if people want the government to act in illiberal ways—by, for example, censoring speech, violating what liberals see as the rights of religious believers, taking private property without just compensation, mandating a particular kind of prayer in schools, or endorsing a particular set of religious convictions—then liberals will stand in opposition. Liberals work to prevent illiberal practices. Sometimes they endanger their lives in doing so. (My father fought in World War II, as an officer in the United States Navy, and he almost lost his life during brutal fighting in the Philippines. He was defending liberal values. He was a liberal. He was a political conservative, by the way.)

73. Some people (mostly on the left) think that because liberals believe in private property, they cannot accept redistribution, or cannot prevent economic inequality from leading to political inequality. Different liberals have different views on these questions. Some liberals insist, at once, on the importance of private property and the need for large-scale redistribution (preferably through the income tax). Nothing in liberalism is incompatible with redistribution to those who need help, and indeed, many liberals believe that the best forms of liberalism require such redistribution (see chapter 7).

74. Because liberals believe in self-government, they are strongly committed to political equality, and seek to ensure it. They are aware that doing so raises serious challenges. They disagree about campaign finance laws and about a host of efforts to promote political equality. Their disagreements are often about the likely effects of such laws and efforts.

75. Liberals believe in kindness, humility, and considerateness.[39] They like this statement, often attributed to Lincoln: "I don't like that man. I must get to know him better." Liberals know that kindness, humility, and considerateness can be challenging to cultivate.

76. Some people (mostly on the right) think that liberals oppose traditions, or treat traditions cavalierly, and that liberalism should be rejected for that reason.[40] In their view, liberals are disrespectful of traditions and want to destroy them. Liberals are baffled by that claim. Consider just a few inherited ideals, norms, and concepts that (many) liberals have defended, often successfully, in the face of focused attack for decades: republican self-government, checks and balances, freedom of speech, freedom of religion, freedom from unreasonable searches and seizures, due process of law, equal protection, the rule of law, private property. Many liberals honor and

cherish the many traditions that define nonpolitical life, whether they involve family, community, or religion.

77. Liberalism's proponents are fully able to defend inherited political ideals and norms, and they often do so. To be sure, they do not think it *adequate* to say that an ideal has been in place for a long time. As Oliver Wendell Holmes Jr. put it: "It is revolting to have no better reason for a rule of law than that so it was laid down in the time of Henry IV. It is still more revolting if the grounds upon which it was laid down have vanished long since, and the rule simply persists from blind imitation of the past."[41] Still, liberals agree that if an ideal has been with us for a long time, there might be a lot to say in its favor. Both Hayek and Burke offered powerful arguments on that count, and nothing in liberalism is inconsistent with their arguments.[42] In fact, many liberals embrace them.

78. Some antiliberals (again, mostly on the right) argue that societies need not only freedom but also constraints. They emphasize the value of community and the need for norms of self-restraint. Most liberals agree with them. They do not favor an atomized society or the disintegration of family, local communities, and social bonds. Many liberals insist that family, local communities, and social bonds are essential.

79. Liberals do not believe that it is a good idea for people to restrict themselves to the pursuit of wealth, pleasure, and power. They believe in the public interest and the common good. The norm of considerateness, for example, is central, and it helps people to live with one another.[43] Liberals famously call for prohibitions on harm to others, but they know that social norms do much more than that.[44] Liberals emphasize the value and importance of constraints on individual choice via both norms and law.[45] Social norms might, for example, combat alcohol abuse and other forms of self-harm. Liberals also care about institutions; they are institutionalists, even if they are willing or eager to consider reforms to plenty of institutions.

80. Many liberals insist on the difference between liberty and license and on the importance of finding ways to combat self-destructive behavior.[46] Consider, for example, restrictions on smoking or bans on the use of dangerous drugs.[47] (More on this in chapter 6.) But liberals believe that constraints on freedom must be justified, and that some justifications, pointing vaguely and abstractly to (say) the will of the sovereign or the public interest, are not enough.

81. Liberals insist on reason-giving in the public domain.[48] They see reason-giving as a check on authoritarianism. They know that authoritarians feel free to exercise power and to use force without justifying their choices.

82. The liberal commitment to reason-giving is closely related to the liberal commitment to deliberative democracy. Public power cannot be exercised only on the ground that "the king says so," "the president says so," or "God says so"—or, even, "the people say so."

83. Liberals do not believe that their own approach is frozen in time. They emphasize that liberalism is being made, not found. They are optimistic about posterity. They do not fear change. In their view, liberalism is not like a rock; it is constantly growing, like a tree.

84. What John Dewey said of the United States is also true of liberalism: "Be the evils what they may, the experiment is not yet played out. The United States are not yet made; they are not a finished fact to be categorically assessed."[49]

85. William F. Buckley Jr. famously said that his preferred form of conservatism "stands athwart history, yelling Stop."[50] Liberals ask history to explain its plans, and if the explanation is good enough, they are prepared to whisper, "Go."

2 EXPERIMENTS OF LIVING

My first sustained exposure to political ideas came from one person, just mentioned: William F. Buckley Jr., who is often taken as the founder of the modern conservative movement in the United States. I was about fourteen years old, and my focus had been on baseball (the beloved Boston Red Sox—Carl Yastrzemski!), basketball (the even more beloved Boston Celtics—Bill Russell!), and, increasingly, women and girls (above all, perhaps, the amazing, unforgettable Elizabeth Montgomery, star of *Bewitched*). I knew about the Vietnam War, of course, and the civil rights movement, and Martin Luther King Jr., who seemed like a hero, but a bit abstract, at least to teenage me.

Somehow, I came across Buckley, and everything changed.

"ONE CANNOT EXAGGERATE INFINITY"

He was dashing and funny. He was devastatingly clever. He was full of charm. He was mischievous. He seemed to know everything. And how the man could write! I subscribed to *National Review*, the magazine he founded. From the mission statement: "There never was an age of conformity quite like this one, or a camaraderie quite like the Liberals'."[1] And this: "Conservatives in this country—at least those who have not made their peace with the New Deal, and there is serious question whether there are others—are non-licensed nonconformists; and this is dangerous business in a Liberal world."[2] And this: "Radical conservatives in this country have an interesting time of it, for when they are not being suppressed or mutilated by the

Liberals, they are being ignored or humiliated by a great many of those of the well-fed Right, whose ignorance and amorality have never been exaggerated for the same reason that one cannot exaggerate infinity."[3] It took teenage me a little time to figure that out, but when I did, I was dazzled.

In the face of all that ignorance and amorality, Buckley had good news: "Our political economy and our high-energy industry run on large, general principles, on ideas—not by day-to-day guess work, expedients and improvisations."[4] He gave you a sense that you could join a club of people—the conservatives—who were smarter than everyone else, and cooler, too. If you joined that club, you'd be a rebel with a cause. And you'd be laughing all the while.

I wrote Buckley a letter. It must have been embarrassing, fawning, idiotic. And you know what? He responded. He wrote me back! I kept that letter—handwritten, as I recall—in my drawer of sacred things.

I read everything I could find by Buckley. The world was in a struggle, I learned, between liberals and conservatives. Liberals were humorless, bumbling, and high-handed. They didn't have a clue. Conservatives knew the secrets. They were woke.

As it happens, a lot of other people were taken with William F. Buckley Jr., too. More than anyone else, Buckley was responsible for the rise of political conservatism in the period between 1950 and the present. He did not only popularize conservative thought; he defined it. Ronald Reagan was a massive fan, and Reaganism had a great deal to do with Buckleyism. Here is what President Reagan said at the thirtieth anniversary dinner of the National Review: "The man standing before you was a Democrat when he picked up his first issue in a plain brown wrapper; and even now, as an occupant of public housing, he awaits as anxiously as ever for his biweekly edition—without the wrapper."[5]

LIBERALISM, FREE MARKETS, RELIGION

Buckley's first book, written soon after his graduation from Yale University, remains a classic, and it helped to establish conservatism in North America and Europe. *God and Man at Yale* levied two attacks on Yale.[6] First, its faculty consisted of socialists. They did not like free markets, which meant that they did not like freedom. Second, its faculty consisted of atheists. They had contempt for religion. Buckley came to *define* liberalism as hostility to freedom and to Christianity. In his conception, conservatism prized both. Indeed, its embrace of Christianity was closely connected with its enthusiasm for free markets and freedom. Christians cherished individual dignity and therefore liberty. Buckley was famous for championing *fusionism*, by which conservatives claimed support from people with disparate commitments: liberty lovers, or libertarians, who loved free markets; religious conservatives, who thought that their faith was under siege; and national security enthusiasts, who emphasized the threat from the Soviet Union. These disparate commitments continue to define conservatism today, with national security enthusiasts emphasizing threats from China and Iran as well as Russia, and with immigration moving to the fore as a serious threat.

Buckley placed a large premium on economic liberty. Let's listen to him:[7]

- "Direct politically the economic activity of a nation, and the economy will lose its capacity for that infinite responsiveness to individual tastes that gives concrete expression to the individual will in material matters."[8]
- "Centralize the political function, and you will lose touch with reality, for the reality is an intimate and individualized relationship between individuals and those among whom they live; and the abstractions of wide-screen social draftsmen will not substitute for it."[9]
- "Stifle the economic sovereignty of the individual by spending his dollars for him, and you stifle his freedom."[10]

Much of the time, Buckley sounded like a classical liberal, a follower of Hayek, who could have agreed with all of those statements.[11] In Buckley's view, the "indicated course of action . . . is to maintain and wherever possible enhance the freedom of the individual to acquire property and dispose of that property in ways that he decides on."[12] James J. Kilpatrick, part of Buckley's stable of writers at *National Review*, wrote simply: "My old-fashioned view is that there is too much 'authority' exerted by government over the lives of free Americans . . . The libertarian ideal, which is a vision I happen to share, cannot be served by extension of 'authority,' but only by a more steadfast devotion to those peculiarly American doctrines of individual liberty which are most dear to me."[13] On this view, Franklin Delano Roosevelt's New Deal was a terrible misstep (see chapter 7).

Buckley despised what he called *Liberalism*, and he spent most of his career railing against it. But all of these propositions grow directly out of the liberal tradition. Was Buckley a liberal? Mostly. He capitalized *Liberalism*, as a dominant approach to politics, so as to distinguish it from *liberalism*, which he knew was different. Insofar as he prized free markets, he reflected that strand of the liberal tradition that is exemplified by Milton Friedman, Ludwig von Mises, Robert Nozick, and of course Hayek himself. You might well conclude that in North America and Europe, many conservatives are liberals.

Indeed, liberalism is what they seek to conserve. The opposition between Buckley's despised Liberals and Buckleyism was heated, but it was a struggle between liberals. Reagan, whom Buckley helped to propel, was a liberal, and Franklin Delano Roosevelt was a liberal as well.

BUCKLEY AND BURKE

All this is true, but we have to introduce some complications. Buckley was not particularly excited about democracy. Individual rights, including the rights to freedom of contract and private property, yes; religious liberty, yes; voting rights, not so much. More precisely, he did not want to extend the franchise so broadly. He believed that it should be restricted to people with high levels of education and ability. He was not at all in favor of a Voting Rights Act. Actually he was against it. Does that mean he was not a liberal? Maybe not, but things are not so clear. Many people in the liberal tradition, including Mill himself, have not favored a universal franchise. I say this even though Lincoln seems to me to have captured liberalism's logic, and it calls for broad voting rights.

There is also the question of traditions. Buckley venerated them. He opposed long-standing practices to the fly-by-night—the latest fad or fashion. In this respect, at least, he was a Burkean. In a particularly vivid passage, Burke writes:

> We wished at the period of the Revolution, and do now wish, to derive all we possess as *an inheritance from our forefathers*. . . . The science of government being therefore so practical in itself, and intended for such practical purposes, a matter which requires experience, and even more experience than any person can gain in his whole life, however sagacious and observing he may be, it is with infinite caution that any man ought to venture upon pulling down an edifice which has answered in any tolerable degree, for ages the common purposes of society, or on building it up again, without having models and patterns of approved utility before his eyes.[14]

Thus Burke stresses the need to rely on experience and in particular the experience of generations. He objects to "pulling down an edifice," a metaphor capturing the understanding of social practices as reflecting the judgments of numerous people extending over time. It is for this reason that Burke describes the "spirit of innovation" as "the result of a selfish temper and confined views,"[15] and offers the term *prejudice* as one of enthusiastic approval, noting that "instead of casting away all our old prejudices, we cherish them to a very considerable degree."[16]

Why, exactly, would prejudices appeal to Burke? The word itself supplies an answer. Prejudices operate before judgment; they supply answers that antedate individual reflection. If prejudices are rooted in long-standing practices, it should not be surprising to find that Burke trusts them. Emphasizing the critical importance of stability, Burke adds a reference to "the evils of inconstancy and versatility, ten thousand times worse than those of obstinacy and the blindest prejudice."[17] All this does not sound so liberal.

Burke's sharpest distinction, then, is between established practices and individual reason. He contends that reasonable citizens, aware of their own limitations, will effectively delegate decision-making authority to their own traditions. "We are afraid to put men to live and trade each on his own private stock of reason," simply "because we suspect that this stock in each man is small, and that the individuals would do better to avail themselves of the general bank and capital of nations, and of ages. Many of our men of speculation, instead of exploding general prejudices, employ their sagacity to discover the latent wisdom which prevails in them."[18]

Buckley seemed to think in these general terms. He liked traditions a lot. If he did not have anything nice to say about *prejudices*, it may have been because the word did not have lovely connotations during the period of the civil rights movement. But he was contemptuous of what he saw as the Liberal enthusiasm for the supposed wisdom of the moment.

Let's put Liberals to one side. On those counts, was Buckley illiberal? Not necessarily. Burke's keen enthusiasm for traditions is grating for liberals; but still, Burkeans might be liberals. Burkeans might be liberals because they are Burkeans. North American traditions are liberal traditions, and the same is true, in the main, for European traditions. Still, the liberal tradition tends to be cautious about traditions. Liberals might cherish them, but they do not revere them. Liberals do not devalue the "private stock of wisdom." They like Spartacus, Galileo, Rosa Parks, and James Dean. They like rebels.

MILL

Consider this emphatically non-Burkean passage from Mill's *On Liberty*:

> That mankind are not infallible; that their truths, for the most part, are only half-truths; that unity of opinion, unless resulting from the fullest and freest comparison of opposite opinions, is not desirable, and diversity not an evil, but a good, until mankind are much more capable than at present of recognising all sides of the truth, are principles applicable to men's modes of action, not less than to their opinions. As it is useful that while mankind are imperfect there should be different opinions, so it is that there should be different experiments of living; that free scope should be given to varieties of character, short of injury to others; and that the worth of different modes of life should be proved practically, when any one thinks fit to try them. It is desirable, in short, that in things which do not primarily concern others, individuality should assert itself. Where, not the person's own character, but the traditions or customs of other people are the rule of conduct, there is wanting one of the principal ingredients of human happiness, and quite the chief ingredient of individual and social progress.[19]

For liberals, these are defining words, a kind of cri de coeur. Mill favored, as the basis for "the rule of conduct," a person's "own character," and he opposed it to "the traditions or customs of other people." Let us underline this sentence: "As it is useful that while mankind are imperfect there should be different opinions, so it is that there should be different experiments of living." The basic idea is that different experiments are beneficial both for individuals and for societies as a whole. People learn from their own experiments, even if they defy traditions; they find out what is best or most meaningful. So too, people can learn from the experiments of others. Perhaps those experiments offer new models. Perhaps they provide examples of ignominious failure. Perhaps they inspire new experiments. The liberal interest in experiments of living is connected to the liberal opposition to conformity. Recall that liberals abhor the unanimity of the graveyard. And a few more words from Mill:

> In this age, the mere example of non-conformity, the mere refusal to bend the knee to custom, is itself a service. Precisely because the tyranny of opinion is such as to make eccentricity a reproach, it is desirable, in order to break through that tyranny, that people should be eccentric. Eccentricity has always abounded when and where strength of character has abounded; and the amount of eccentricity in a society has generally been proportional to the amount of genius, mental vigor, and moral courage which it contained. That so few now dare to be eccentric, marks the chief danger of the time.[20]

Liberals do not like the idea of bending the knee, whether to a leader, an employer, or a custom. (Recall Bob Dylan: "Even the president of the United States sometimes must have to stand naked.") They welcome eccentricity. Might the idea of experiments of living help ground political practice? Might it lie at the foundations of the best forms of liberalism? I think so.

Here is a proposal, for your consideration: *experiments of living constitutionalism*. We can understand the idea of *constitutionalism* both figuratively and literally. In its figurative sense, we might see a commitment to experiments of living as undergirding political practice. A liberal nation might say: We protect a wide range of experiments. If it says that, it is offering a defining commitment, a kind of promise. The commitment need not have the same kind of status as a formal constitutional commitment. It might simply be understood as a background principle of a liberal regime.

In its literal sense, we might understand a commitment to experiments of living as having a more formal constitutional status. When the government does not permit people to experiment, it presumptively violates their constitutional rights. Of course it is true that there are experiments and there are experiments: People do not have a constitutional right to experiment with different ways of murdering or raping people, or different means of creating weapons of mass destruction. Some experiments are intolerable or beyond the pale. (Which ones? A good question, and there are different liberal answers.) The basic idea is that so long as they are not harming others, and across a wide terrain, people can speak as they like, associate as they like, organize as they like, live as they like, and worship as they like, without interference from government.[21] It follows that the United States Constitution, and other constitutions too, should be interpreted to allow both individuals and groups to experiment with different ways of living, whether we are speaking of religious practices, child-rearing, family arrangements, romance, schooling, or work. Experiments of living constitutionalism prizes diversity and plurality; it opposes (what it sees as) authoritarianism in all its forms.

Drawing on Mill's conception of liberalism, experiments of living constitutionalism insists on the importance of allowing and encouraging "varieties of character" and on the value of "different modes of life." It does so in part because it values the dignity of every individual, who should be entitled to find his or her own way. It does so in part because it sees experiments of living as essential to social as well as individual progress. If each of us is able to see what each of us has tried, we will have more options to consider; all of us will be able to learn from each of us. Unsuccessful experiments of living may be nothing to celebrate, but they contribute to both individual and social progress. For those who embrace experiments of living constitutionalism, experiments of living also contribute to the public interest and the common good.

There are other reasons to endorse experiments of living constitutionalism. If a nation allows experiments of living, it increases the chance that diverse people will be able to live together. In a sense, it adopts an arms control agreement: You can embark on your experiment so long as I can embark on mine. At the same time, experiments of living constitutionalism promotes the liberal value of security, or freedom from fear.

FREEDOMS

Consistent with the account in chapter 1, those who favor experiments of living constitutionalism believe that freedom of speech is the most fundamental right of all. They see it as a way of identifying experiments of living, both by projecting them imaginatively and by publicizing those that are actually in motion. They embrace Justice Robert Jackson's words, which, it will be recalled, were quoted in chapter 1: "Compulsory unification of opinion achieves only the unanimity of the graveyard."[22] They also agree with his suggestion: "If there is any fixed star in our constitutional constellation, it is that no official, high or petty, can prescribe what shall be orthodox in politics, nationalism, religion, or other matters of opinion or force citizens to confess by word or act their faith therein."[23]

To be sure, they do not believe that the first amendment is "an absolute." (See chapter 5.) They know that some speech contributes little or nothing to experiments of living, and they know that some speech imposes serious and immediate harm. They do not think it is a legitimate experiment of living for someone to say, "Your money or your life." They would allow restrictions on bribery, perjury, and fraud, and they would permit restrictions on free speech when there is a clear and present danger. But they would resist efforts to authorize any kind of censorship of political dissent or the arts.

In the same vein, those who favor experiments of living constitutionalism prize freedom of religion. They would allow a plurality of faiths to flourish. They would vigorously protect people of faith, agnostics, and atheists. They would stand in the way of federal or state efforts to impose secular values, even widely held ones, on people whose religious traditions are inconsistent with those values. For related reasons, experiments of living constitutionalists have no problem with home schooling and the idea of a constitutional right, held by parents, to make choices with respect to their children's education.[24]

Experiments of living constitutionalists are enthusiastic about freedom of association, whether we are speaking of civic associations, political associations, religious associations, or associations of some other kind. Those who favor experiments of living constitutionalism would also be strongly inclined to protect contemporary rights of privacy, including the right to use contraceptives, the right to live with members of one's family,[25] the right to engage in consensual sodomy,[26] and the right to same-sex marriage. For those who embrace experiments of living constitutionalism, the focus on sexual privacy is not a mistake, a coincidence, or some kind of indulgence (see chapter 3). It is entirely appropriate and something to be celebrated, for sex is emphatically a domain in which "individuality should assert itself." (Within limits, of course, above all to protect children.)

Experiments of living constitutionalism takes the right to choose abortion seriously, but those who embrace experiments greatly struggle with that issue. For them, it is not an easy question; the moral issue is difficult. (My experiment of living does not allow me to hurt you.) Those who embrace experiments of living might not commit themselves to a right to choose, because of the importance and the value of protecting human life. Infanticide is not a permissible experiment in living. Following liberal principles, as elaborated by Mill and others, those who believe in experiments of living would not allow harm to others. Reasonable people, committed to experiments of living constitutionalism, disagree about whether abortion can be counted as that. (They also disagree about whether and to what extent people can be restrained even when there is no harm to others— consider alcohol abuse—and about how to understand the very category of harm to others. These are hard questions.)

Experiments of living constitutionalism is a great friend to federalism, seeing the diversity of the states as an engine for the creation of experiments of living. Local norms and cultures deserve protection (unless they squelch, through government, experiments of living). Those who embrace experiments of living constitutionalism much like the idea of *laboratories of democracy*; they will strongly resist efforts to override values and approaches that are prized by citizens of (for example) California, Mississippi, or Wyoming.[27] They will not be inclined to favor national preemption of state law.

At the same time, they will be open-minded on separation of powers questions; the commitment to experiments of living constitutionalism does not entail a particular approach to grants of discretion to administrative agencies, or to the idea of a unitary president. But that commitment does entail approaching those issues with Mill's cautionary note in mind: "Where, not the person's own character, but the traditions or customs of other people are the rule of conduct, there is wanting one of the principal ingredients of human happiness, and quite the chief ingredient of individual and social progress."[28]

As its name (accidentally!) suggests, experiments of living constitutionalism is a form of living constitutionalism. Its advocates are skeptical of originalism, as reflected in the idea that the Constitution should be understood in accordance with its original public meaning. But experiments of living constitutionalists believe that their preferred approach has deep roots in Anglo-American traditions (and also in important traditions in Europe, Asia, and Africa), and that it can be understood in a way that is faithful to the text of the U.S. Constitution.

PEDIGREE

At this point, you might have numerous questions. What is the pedigree of experiments of living constitutionalism? Where does it come from? Does the U.S. Constitution enact John Stuart Mill's *On Liberty*? Does any nation's constitution really do that? Those who embrace experiments of living constitutionalism think that they can answer these questions. They believe that their defining ideals are rooted in the distinctive form of liberal republicanism that defined and launched many contemporary constitutions, including the United States Constitution.[29] In brief: liberal republicanism is liberal insofar as it emphasizes the agency and dignity of all of us; it is both liberal and republican insofar as it sees government as an engine for collective deliberation about the public good.

Experiments of living constitutionalists claim continuity with liberal republicanism. They believe that Mill was both summarizing and broadening principles, rooted in the liberal tradition and also congenial to republicanism, that predated and informed the American founding. They insist that the Fourteenth and Fifteenth Amendments are animated by a commitment to freedom that fits comfortably with experiments of living constitutionalism. In their view, the idea of experiments of living has a long tradition behind it; Montesquieu and Locke defended versions of that idea, as did Madison, Hamilton, and Jefferson. Mill was hardly writing on a clean slate; the idea of experiments of living is anything but a bolt from the blue.

In American constitutional law, Justice Oliver Wendell Holmes Jr. spoke directly in the terms of experiments of living constitutionalism in his great dissenting opinion in *Abrams v. United States*, decided in 1919:

> But when men have realized that time has upset many fighting faiths, they may come to believe even more than they believe the very foundations of their own conduct that the ultimate good desired is better reached by free trade in ideas—that the best test of truth is the power of the thought to get itself accepted in the competition of the market, and that truth is the only ground upon which their wishes safely can be carried out. That at any rate is the theory of our Constitution. It is an experiment, as all life is an experiment. Every year if not every day we have to wager our salvation upon some prophecy based upon imperfect knowledge. While that experiment is part of our system I think that we should be eternally vigilant against attempts to check the expression of opinions that we loathe and believe to be fraught with death, unless they so imminently threaten immediate interference with the lawful and pressing purposes of the law that an immediate check is required to save the country.[30]

Skeptics might ask how experiments of living constitutionalism relates to any existing constitution, and whether it promises, or threatens, to produce radical reforms. Would government paternalism, understood as the displacement of individual choices by officials who think they know best, be out of bounds? Always? Would motorcycle helmet laws be out of bounds? Would there be a right to polygamous marriages? To incestuous marriages? To pornography? These are fair and challenging questions. In response, defenders of experiments of living constitutionalism have four things to say.

First, they are not fanatics, and they need not embrace everything that Mill says about liberty. Certainly they need not go so far as to accept Mill's harm principle (which, it will be recalled, forbids regulation unless it is justified as a way of preventing harm to others; see chapter 5). You can believe in experiments of living constitutionalism without thinking that government paternalism, even of the coercive sort, is always out of bounds. Experiments of living constitutionalists should have no trouble with laws that require people to buckle their seat belts, to wear helmets while riding motorcycles, or to save money for retirement (as through Social Security). They can accept cigarette taxes, even if the goal of such taxes is to prevent people from harming themselves. Nor would they have much interest in the view that the Constitution protects a right to polygamous marriages, incestuous marriages, or child pornography.

One reason is that in some of these cases, individual choices clearly impose harm to others (consider child pornography). If your experiment injures someone else, you had better stop experimenting. And even when people are not harming others, experiments of living constitutionalists insist, as Mill did not, on the importance of distinguishing between genuine experiments of living that are fundamental to people's lives (as when people choose to live together in lieu of marriage, or follow a religious conviction of their own) and choices that clearly lack that character (as when people decide not to buckle their seat belts, or not to save for retirement). To be sure, there might be some hard line–drawing problems here.

Second, experiments of living constitutionalists emphasize that far from being radical, their approach helps to clarify and support a great deal of existing Anglo-American law, much of which rests on liberal foundations. Since the 1960s, for example, the United States Supreme Court has vigorously protected freedom of speech, including not only political speech but also literature, art, cinema, and much more. (The court is largely following Holmes.) In the process, it has also protected a great deal of sexually explicit speech. So too, freedom of association enjoys broad protection. So does religious liberty. As noted, the justices have ruled that sexual privacy qualifies for protection under the due process clause. It is not simple to produce an account that explains and supports all these disparate rulings. Experiments of living constitutionalism can provide such an account. (Something broadly similar could be said about Canada, Ireland, Germany, the United Kingdom, and many other nations.)

Third, defenders of experiments of living constitutionalism are willing to be respectful of precedents and traditions, whether or not they agree with them. They may not agree, for example, with the court's ruling that the Constitution does not protect the right to physician-assisted suicide.[31] But like almost everyone else, they do not think it appropriate to overrule decisions and long-standing practices simply because they believe that they were wrong. You can accept experiments of living constitutionalism while also thinking that any legal system on earth needs to respect stare decisis, so as to prevent instability and perhaps even a form of constitutional chaos. A legal or political system cannot operate if today's decision is in tomorrow's garbage heap.

Fourth, those who embrace experiments of living constitutionalism would give careful attention to the decisions of democratic processes. They are liberals, after all, and liberals are democrats, even if there are real limits on what democracies can do. Experiments of living constitutionalists will have to make some difficult choices here, but if Congress or a state legislature has made a reasonable decision, supporters of experiments of living constitutionalism might well be cautious before rejecting it. You can believe in experiments of living without being a fanatic. Everything depends on the details—on the kind of liberty that is at stake, and on the strength of the argument for interfering with it.

A TIME-HONORED CHALLENGE, AND NORMS

Some critics of the idea of experiments of living, and of liberalism in general, are highly skeptical of claims of this sort. (Buckley himself would be intensely critical.) We have seen that many liberals, and many antiliberals, insist that liberal societies cannot work without sentiments, norms, and institutions that precede individual choice. Candidates include attachments to family, community, heritage, God, or nation. Since the early eighteenth century, liberals have been both committed to and troubled by that claim. Constant was committed to it; Tocqueville was troubled by it. As a representative example, consider this set of claims about "the moral and anthropological status of human beings":

> 1) Men and women are religious and spiritual creatures . . . 2) Men and women are born into preexisting social, religious, and economic institutions and customs; 3) Many of these institutions and customs are naturally hierarchical and unequal but are nevertheless interconnected, spanning the sacred and temporal worlds; and 4) Men and women bear moral obligations to their fellow man that are not the product of subjective consent and preference.
>
> These insights are the closest thing to fixed—and apolitical—truths as any concerning the human condition. It is thus difficult to provide a persuasive defense of any political or intellectual tradition without validating them.[32]

On one view, liberalism cannot survive or flourish without antiliberal or preliberal attachments, customs, and institutions. Without the family, communal attachments, and religion, people may indeed be choosers; but they are unanchored, rootless, lost.

Those who believe in experiments of living, and in liberalism, might respond gently and modestly to arguments of this kind. They might acknowledge the possibility that the various claims are right. They might add that if the claims are indeed right, a society that embraces liberalism, and that allows experiments of living, will be almost certainly pervaded by those very attachments, institutions, norms, and customs. They might add that while liberalism itself does not require or mandate the relevant attachments, norms, institutions, or customs, it certainly makes space for them, and it vigorously protects them. Indeed, experiments of living constitutionalism is strongly inclined to give some of them constitutional protection (under the rubric of freedom of association and freedom of religion). Liberals might insist that it is not liberalism's job to cultivate or breed those attachments. That is the job of others.

True enough, or at least plausible enough. But at this point, some skeptics will be deeply unsatisfied. They will respond that by its nature, liberalism tends to devour or destroy the necessary attachments, institutions, and customs. Its emphasis on freedom of choice, and on personal selection of "experiments," will make it hard or impossible for the relevant attachments (to family, God, nation) to survive. The liberal commitment to reasongiving and rationalism compounds the problem. (Do you love your family because it is rational to do?) The likely consequence is a kind of nightmare of freedom, a Millian dystopia, of the sort frequently observed (the critics insist) in liberal societies. Ross Douthat puts it this way: "Where it once delivered equality, liberalism now offers plutocracy; instead of liberty, appetitiveness regulated by a surveillance state; instead of true intellectual and religious freedom, growing conformity and mediocrity. It has reduced rich cultures to consumer products, smashed social and familial relations, and left us all the isolated and mutually suspicious inhabitants of an 'anticulture' from which many genuine human goods have fled."[33]

But the critics are being reckless here. Consider the four claims listed earlier. What exactly do they mean? Are they, in fact, "fixed—and apolitical—truths"? Maybe or maybe not. More fundamentally, the claim that liberalism, in the abstract, devours the kinds of attachments, customs, and institutions on which it depends is an *empirical* claim. Where is the evidence for it? What, exactly, has caused what, specifically? Douthat says that "liberalism" has "reduced rich cultures to consumer products" and "smashed social and familial relations." (It is as if "liberalism" is Voldemort in the Harry Potter novels.) Really? How has liberalism done that? The people who are making the relevant claims are not empiricists. They might be right, or partly right, but they do not really have evidence. They have narratives. They rest content with high-sounding adjectives and nouns, or with intuitively plausible stories, or with empirical claims about trends that have no clear or demonstrable connection with liberalism as such.

Liberalism is not a person. It is not Voldemort. Like Douthat, people who are unfriendly to liberalism on normative grounds make arguments about its social effects, which are said to include a growth in out-of-wedlock childbirth, lower marriage rates, higher divorce rates, repudiation of traditions, economic inequality, deterioration of civic associations, political correctness, hostility or indifference to religion, and a general sense of social alienation and rootlessness. In the abstract, we cannot rule out the possibility that in some sense, "liberalism" is partly responsible for one or another trend, just as we cannot rule out the possibility that the real culprit is misogyny, racism, feminism, capitalism, atheism, political correctness, television, economic growth, modern birth control, the iPhone, Facebook, or the internet. Even so, the idea that "liberalism" is responsible for a decline in social relations, lower marriage rates, same-sex marriage, high rates of economic growth, low rates of economic growth, or speech codes on university campuses is puzzling. It would hardly be enough to observe, for example, that defenders of same-sex marriage invoke something like Mill's harm principle, or that Bentham was enthusiastic about immigration.

But suppose that we do find, in some liberal societies some of the time, increases in crime, decreases in marriage rates, decreases in church attendance, and increases in the rates of children born to single-headed households. Is liberalism responsible for that? What does that even mean? Perhaps it might be said that an emphasis on personal autonomy and individual choice has contributed to some of these things. It is true that if Mill's harm principle rules not only a government but also a culture, we might see a decline in norms of self-control and self-restraint. We could imagine a form of liberalism, emphatic on (say) the pursuit of self-interest and the

gratification of individual desires, that would have corrosive or even hor-
rifying effects. But is that really a form of liberalism? Certainly it is not anything like the best form, or the form that produced liberalism as a political
creed. As we have seen, liberals of multiple kinds have been emphatic on
the importance of social norms, including norms of kindness, considerateness, self-control, and self-restraint. Edna Ullmann-Margalit is just one
example.[34] (If Mill did not emphasize such norms, it is not because he did
not believe in them; it is because he had different targets.)

As we have also seen, liberalism is a work in progress. It is not a finished fact or a *fait accompli*. Contemporary liberals should stress the need to
accompany liberal commitments, including the commitment to autonomy,
with an emphasis on the central importance of civic and personal virtues,
including considerateness,[35] civility, and self-control. Inculcation of those
virtues is not fundamentally a task for government, but government can
play a role (see chapter 5), and it is a fundamental task. It requires a flour-
ishing set of social norms. Consider James Madison's words in the Virginia
Ratifying Convention: "Is there no virtue among us? If there be not, we are
in a wretched situation. No theoretical checks, no form of government, can
render us secure."[36]

We should agree that some experiments of living should be deplored
(consider a life of indolence) and that others should be outlawed (consider
a life of crime). Those who believe in experiments of living constitutionalism embrace these points. They know that the specification of unwelcome,
illegitimate, or intolerable experiments is an essential challenge, and that
liberals can disagree about how best to meet it. They believe in norms.
They have diverse views about which norms are best. They do not welcome harm to others. They might well be comfortable with some efforts
to protect people against harming themselves (consider compulsory seat
belt laws); many liberals disagree with Mill and would allow paternalism
in compelling circumstances (see chapter 5). The only claim, an admittedly
general one, is that governments in free societies should give people a wide
berth—a chance to find their own way.

CHOOSING

How shall we choose between experiments of living constitutionalism and
other approaches? Any answer to that question would have to offer criteria

of selection, which are urgently needed. I suggest that the only possible answer is another question: *What would make a constitutional order better rather than worse?* That is an admittedly daunting question, but there is no alternative to asking it.[37] (It is also the liberal question, though nonliberals should ask it, too.) The U.S. Constitution does not contain the instructions for its own interpretation, and the same is true for constitutions all over the globe.

In the United States, some "originalists," focused on the original public meaning, seem to think that their preferred approach follows from the very idea of interpretation, but it really does not. In the end, originalism has to be justified on the ground that it would make our system better rather than worse. Many alternative approaches, including experiments of living constitutionalism, can fall within the domain of interpretation, so long as they operate by reference to and within the space of the text of the Constitution itself. It is hopeless to defend a contested theory of interpretation by citing the founding document and pounding the table. The only way to defend such a theory, or to evaluate it, is to ask what it would do for the institutions and rights under which people live. Where else can we possibly turn?

To be more specific: in order to choose a theory of constitutional interpretation, judges (and others) must seek *reflective equilibrium*, in which their judgments, at multiple levels of generality, are brought into alignment with one another.[38] In *A Theory of Justice*, a defining liberal text, John Rawls elaborates the basic idea for purposes of moral and political philosophy.[39] He begins with this suggestion: "There are some questions which we feel sure must be answered in a certain way. For example, we are confident that religious intolerance and racial discrimination are unjust."[40] On some issues, we are confident that we "have reached what we believe is an impartial judgment," and the resulting convictions are "provisional fixed points which we presume any conception of justice must fit."[41] At the same time, there are some questions on which we lack clear answers, and our aim might be to "remove our doubts."[42] We might want our "principles to accommodate our firmest convictions and to provide guidance where guidance is needed."[43]

As Rawls understands the matter, fixed points are only provisionally fixed; we might hold some judgment (say, the death penalty is morally unacceptable) with a great deal of confidence, and we might be exceedingly reluctant to give it up. But we should be willing to consider the possibility that we are wrong. In recent decades, many people opposed same-sex marriage quite firmly, but their judgment shifted, in part because their opposition did not fit well with what else they thought, and with the general principles that they hold.

As Rawls understands the matter, "we work from both ends," involving both abstract principles and judgments about particular cases.[44] If some general principles "match our considered convictions" about those cases, there is no problem. In the case of discrepancies, we might "revise our existing judgments" about particular cases, "for even the judgments we take provisionally as fixed points are liable to revision." We go back and forth between principles and judgments. When we produce "principles which match our considered judgments duly pruned and adjusted," we are in "reflective equilibrium," defined as such because "our principles and judgments coincide," because "we know to what principles our judgments conform and the premises of their derivation."[45]

To be sure, the equilibrium might not be *stable*. It might be upset if, for example, reflections "lead us to revise our judgments."[46] It is important to emphasize that on Rawls's account, a "conception of justice cannot be deduced from self-evident premises or conditions on principles"; it is a matter "of everything fitting together into one coherent view."[47] And importantly, Rawls suggests that we consult "our considered convictions at all levels of generality; no one level, say that of abstract principle or that of particular judgments in particular cases, is viewed as foundational. They all may have an initial credibility."[48]

Rawls's motivation was "the hypothesis that the principles which would be chosen in the original position are identical with those that match our considered judgments and so these principles describe our sense of justice."[49] But Rawls urges that this view is too simple, because our considered judgments might be wrong. They might be "subject to certain irregularities and distortions."[50] For example, we might think that meat-eating is acceptable, or that meat-eating is not acceptable, and we cannot know whether we should continue to think that until we test the proposition against our other judgments. When we are given "an intuitively appealing account" of what justice requires, we may well revise our "judgments to conform to its principles even though the theory does not fit" our existing judgments exactly.[51]

Whether or not we agree with Rawls for purposes of moral and political philosophy, there is a close analogy in constitutional law. Theories of constitutional interpretation are standardly defended or rejected, embraced or discarded, by asking how well they fit with our considered judgments at multiple levels of generality. There is no alternative. We cannot know what approach would make our constitutional order better rather than worse without seeking reflective equilibrium. In the United States, most people would be reluctant to accept a theory of interpretation that leads to the conclusion that *Brown v. Board of Education*[52] was wrongly decided. If a proposed theory would allow racial segregation by state governments, the theory might well (in their view, and mine too) have to be rejected for that reason. At the very least, a theory of interpretation that would allow racial segregation must meet a heavy burden of justification.

The reason, in short, is that a constitutional order that allowed racial segregation would be intolerably unjust, and we should not understand our constitutional order to authorize intolerable injustice unless we are required to do so. So long as a theory of interpretation is optional, we should not adopt one that allows intolerable injustice. What is taken as intolerably unjust by some is not so taken by others, which helps explain why different people have different fixed points.

Suppose that a theory would mean that *District of Columbia v. Heller*,[53] protecting the individual right to possess guns, was incorrectly decided. Some people would conclude that if so, the theory is questionable. Many people would think that if a theory suggests that *Brandenburg v. Ohio*,[54] broadly protecting political speech through a version of the "clear and present danger" test, was wrong, then the theory is much less appealing. Other people will think that if a theory suggests that *Brandenburg v. Ohio*, broadly protecting freedom of speech, was right, or might be right, we had better find another theory.

Fixed points might not be limited to *existing* rulings. People care about the constitutional future, not merely the constitutional present. Many people would reject a theory of interpretation that might make space for, or require, a (future) return to *Lochner v. New York*,[55] which struck down maximum hour laws, or anything like it. People might reject a theory of interpretation that might, in the future, allow or require government to restrict political dissent. (Advocates of experiments of living constitutionalism would certainly do that.) One might reject a theory of interpretation that puts the administrative state in (future) constitutional jeopardy, and that would (for example) cast constitutional doubt on the Clean Air Act or the Occupational Safety and Health Act.

More fundamentally, many people would reject a theory of interpretation that would rule out new and (to us) surprising developments that would expand prevailing conceptions of liberty and equality. They would insist on opening the ground for something like a *Brown v. Board of Education*[56] (striking down school segregration), or an *Obergefell*[57] (striking down bans on same-sex marriage), for new and future generations. They would also make a bet that a Supreme Court, operating under a theory that makes space for decisions like *Brown* or *Obergefell*, appropriately expanding equality and liberty, would produce a similar decision in 2030, or 2040, or 2090, also appropriately expanding equality and liberty (not the worst bet, though also perhaps not the best).

In short: judges (and others) must consider the consequences of their choice for particular judgments that operate, for them, as provisional fixed points, understood as judgments that seem both clear and firm. If a theory of interpretation would allow the federal government to discriminate on the basis of race and sex, it is unlikely to be a good theory of interpretation; it is at least presumptively unacceptable for that reason.

I have used the term *provisional fixed points*, and in this respect I am following Rawls, who emphasizes their provisional character in moral and political philosophy. A judge might believe something with real conviction. Even so, a judge ought to be willing to listen to counterarguments; humility is a good thing. Few points are so fixed that nothing at all could dislodge them. Still, people have beliefs about constitutional meaning that would be exceptionally difficult to dislodge. They might have an assortment of such beliefs. What I am urging here is that that is entirely fine. Fixed points about particular cases are central to assessments of theories of constitutional interpretation.

It might be tempting to respond that the choice of a theory of interpretation cannot possibly depend on the results that it yields. One might think that that choice has to be made on the basis of some commitment that might seem higher or more fundamental. If we focus on results, and choose a theory of interpretation on the basis of results, perhaps we are biased, or unforgivably "result-oriented," and engaged in some kind of special pleading.

The problem with that response is that it rests on an illusion of compulsion. Among the reasonable candidates, judges (and others) are not compelled to adopt a particular theory of interpretation; they must make a choice. One more time: to do that, judges (and others) are required to think about what would make our constitutional order better rather than worse. To be sure, we should not consider, as fixed points, only results about particular cases (though they matter a great deal). We must also consider defining ideals (including self-government and the rule of law), and we must think about processes and institutions. There might be fixed points there as well.

Note that there is a large and critical difference between fixed points and preferred results. You might want the Supreme Court to issue certain rulings, but if it does not, you will think it reasonable, and even if you think it unreasonable, you might not think that something horrible or horrific has happened. A theory of constitutional law might not yield *all* of one's preferred results (it had better not!), but it might also yield, or at least not foreclose, all, most, or many of one's fixed points. Note as well that I am suggesting that for judges (or others), thinking about theories of constitutional interpretation, the relevant fixed points really are, and must be, their own. And it is important to see that we are not speaking of a small number of fixed points or a handful of iconic cases; a theory of interpretation might be acceptable if it undoes just a few. The real problem comes if such a theory operates as a wrecking ball. The real question is which theory makes a constitutional order the best that it can be.

Here is a liberal answer to that question: experiments of living constitutionalism.

3 HAYEK AND MILL

Mill and Hayek help to define the liberal tradition, but in both tempera-ment and orientation, they could not be further apart. Mill was a progres-sive, a social reformer, an optimist about change, in some ways a radical. He believed that, properly understood, liberalism calls for significant revisions in the existing economic order, which he saw as palpably unjust: "The most powerful of all the determining circumstances is birth. The great majority are what they were born to be."[1] We will return to that point in chapter 8.

Hayek was not exactly a conservative; in fact, he was sharply critical of conservatism on the ground that it was largely oppositional and did not offer an affirmative position. But he is a hero to many conservatives. One reason is that he generally venerated traditions and long-standing practices, seeing them as embodying the views and knowledge of countless people over long periods. Hayek admired Burke, who (it will be recalled) attacked the idea that self-styled reformers, equipped with an abstract theory, should feel free to override social practices that have stood the test of time. Mill had an abstract theory, one based on a conception of liberty from both govern-ment and oppressive social customs, and he thought that society could be evaluated by reference to it. Understanding Hayek and Mill, and what unifies and separates them, is fundamental to understanding the liberal tradition.

Against this background, there is every reason to be intrigued by a book with the title *Hayek on Mill*.[2] Hayek died in 1992, but the University of Chi-cago Press is continuing to publish a multivolume edition of his collected works. Readers are discovering essays by Hayek that were never published, were not easily available, or were not widely known. What would Hayek have to say about a great champion of liberty, in some ways his intellectual ancestor, who ended up embracing socialism? What would Hayek, one of the great twentieth-century liberals, say about Mill, the greatest nineteenth-century liberal?

How stunning, then, to find that Hayek offered only a few snippets on that question. His treatment, first published in 1951, grew out of an enormous, uncharacteristic, and somewhat obsessive undertaking. Startlingly, Hayek assembled what remains of the correspondence between Mill and his eventual wife, Harriet Taylor (one or the other destroyed numerous letters, probably including the most interesting), and used it as the basis for a narrative account of their mysterious love affair.

The book raises mysteries of its own. For all his greatness, Hayek was a cold, abstract, and distant writer, celebrating the operations of free markets but without a lot of interest in the full range of human emotions. Was he passionate? In a way, about markets and the rule of law (as he understood it). Some liberals, including Mill, have a romantic streak; Hayek did not. How was it, exactly, that Hayek, of all people, became captivated by the story of John Stuart Mill and Harriet Taylor? One answer is that he had to explain to himself and others why Mill—one of the few thinkers he had to regard as an intellectual equal or superior—moved away from what Hayek celebrated as classical liberalism, which for Hayek was focused on limited government and protection of free markets. But Hayek's interest in the romance itself outpaced his interest in the evolution of Mill's thinking (perhaps because of the beauty and great delicacy of the correspondence). Hayek's personal life, which had a stormy romance of its own, might help account for his interest in Mill's romance. Still, Mill was a romantic liberal, seeing liberalism itself as a kind of romance; Hayek was anything but that, and he saw liberalism as anything but that.

Does Mill's relationship with Harriet Taylor have anything to do with liberalism and liberty? I think so. One of the lessons we can draw from Hayek's work of excavation is that Mill's distinctive form of liberalism, with its emphasis on individual freedom from the confining effect of social norms, owed a large debt to his relationship with Taylor. As we shall see, Hayek himself missed the connection entirely, because his own preoccupations lay elsewhere.

Hayek begins with one of his central puzzles, and it involves Taylor rather than Mill: "The literary portrait which in the *Autobiography* John

Stuart Mill has drawn for us of the woman who ultimately became his wife creates a strong wish to know more about her."[3] Mill's own account suggests, with evident skepticism, that she must have been "one of the most remarkable women who ever lived." Hayek quotes a very long passage from Mill himself:

> In general spiritual characteristics, as well as in temperament and organization, I have often compared her, as she was at this time, to Shelley: but in thought and intellect, Shelley, so far as his powers were developed in his short life, was but a child compared with what she ultimately became. Alike in the highest regions of speculation and in the smaller practical concerns of daily life, her mind was the same perfect instrument, piercing to the very heart and marrow of the matter; always seizing the essential idea or principle. The same exactness and rapidity of operation, pervading as it did her sensitive as [well as] her mental faculties, would with her gifts of feeling and imagination have fitted her to be a consummate artist, as her fiery and tender soul and her vigourous eloquence would certainly have made her a great orator, and her profound knowledge of human nature and discernment and sagacity in practical life, would in [the] times when such a *carrière* was open to women, have made her eminent among the rulers of mankind.[4]

Mill had a lot more to say about Harriet Taylor: "Were I [but] capable of interpreting to the world one half the great thoughts and noble feelings which are buried in her grave, I should be the medium of a greater benefit to it, than is ever likely to arise from anything that I can write, unprompted and unassisted by her all but unrivalled wisdom."[5] One of Hayek's projects is to discover whether Mill's account was "sheer delusion."[6]

Mill and Taylor met at a dinner in 1830, when she was just twenty-two, a mother of two boys, and married for four years to John Taylor, eleven years older than she and a junior partner in a family firm of wholesale druggists. Thomas Carlyle called him "an innocent dull good man."[7] An acquaintance describes her, at the time, as "possessed of a beauty and grace quite unique of their kind," with "large dark eyes, not soft or sleepy, but with a look of quiet command in them."[8] (The best words here are *grace* and *quiet command*.) She wrote poetry and was soon to produce a number of essays on social usages and conventions, including one that strongly prefigured Mill's attacks on conformity, decades later, in *On Liberty*.[9]

For his part, Mill was nothing like the dry, somewhat desiccated old man depicted in photographs. Twenty-four at the time, he must have cut a dashing figure, having been described by Carlyle as "a slender, rather tall and elegant youth," who was "remarkably gifted with precision of utterance, enthusiastic, yet lucid, calm."[10] At the same time, his emotional state was not good. In a forlorn letter to a friend, written a year before meeting Taylor, he referred to "the comparative loneliness of my probable future lot," and contended that there was "now no human being . . . who acknowledges a common object with me."[11]

In his autobiography, Mill insisted that it was not until years after meeting Taylor that their relationship "became at all intimate or confidential."[12] Hardly. Referring to an article published in mid-1831, Taylor's closest friend pointedly wrote her, "Did you or Mill do it?"[13] In the same year, a letter from a mutual friend, written to John Taylor, spoke mysteriously of the need for a "reconciliation" between Mr. Taylor and Mill.[14] In 1832, Mrs. Taylor wrote Mill that they must not meet again, to which Mill responded in French: "Sa route et la mienne sont séparées, elle l'a dit: mais elles peuvent, elles doivent, se rencontrer. A quelqu' époque, dans quelqu' endroit, que ce puisse être, elle me trouvera toujours ce que j'ai été, ce que je suis encore."[15] ("Her path and mine are separate, she said so: but they can, they must, come together. At whatever time, in whatever place that might be, she will find me forever as I was, as I am still." If you have ever been in a real romance, those words will speak directly to you.) A few weeks later, their relationship resumed.

By 1832, the two had embarked on some kind of love affair. Taylor wrote Mill: "Far from being unhappy or even *low* this morning, I feel as tho' you had never loved me half so well as last night."[16] And later, in response to an apparent confession from Mill:

> I am glad that you have said it—I am *happy* that you have—no one with any fineness & beauty of character but must feel compelled to say *all*, to the being they really *love*, or rather with any *permanent* reservation it is *not* love—while there is reservation, however little of it, the love is just *so much* imperfect. . . . *Yes*—these circumstances *do* require greater strength than any other—the greatest—that which you have, & which if you had not I should never have loved you, I should not love you now.[17]

The Taylors agreed to a separation, and Mill and Harriet were able to spend time together. To a close friend, Mill wrote a rapturous letter: "I am astonished when I think how much has been restrained, how much untold, unshewn and uncommunicated till now. . . . Not a day has passed without removing some real & serious obstacle to happiness. . . . There will never again I believe be any obstacle to our being together entirely."[18] Taylor wrote in a similar spirit, stating that "there has been so much more pain than I thought I was capable of, but also O how much more happiness."[19]

Hayek writes that in the middle of the 1830s, Mill and Taylor did not try to conceal their intimacy, but confronted with a great deal of malicious gossip, they withdrew almost entirely from social life. In 1834, Carlyle wrote of the rumor that Mill had "fallen *desperately in love* with some young philosophic beauty" and been "lost to all his friends and to himself."[20] Enraged by the gossip, Mill cut off a number of his friendships. He wrote to a friend: "What ought to be so much easier to me than to her, is in reality more difficult—costs harder struggle—to part company with the opinion of the world, and with my former mode of doing good in it."[21] You might reasonably speculate that Mill's eventual writing on conformity, and on the importance of individuality, had some connection with his personal experiences.

It is not entirely clear what happened between Mill and Taylor from the middle of the 1830s to the late 1840s. What little that remains of their correspondence shows a degree of agitation within and between them. Wrote Taylor to Mill: "I don't know why I was so low when you went this morning. I was *so* low—I could not bear your going my darling one; yet I should be well enough accustomed to it by now."[22] The two were alert to the reactions of others; Mill seemed especially sensitive on that count. Wrote Taylor to Mill, perhaps teasingly: "I was not *quite* wrong in thinking you feared opinions.— I never supposed you dreaded the opinions of fools but only of those who are otherwise wise & good but have not your opinions about Moralities."[23] But there can be little doubt about the intensity of their relationship. Wrote Taylor to Mill: "When I think that I shall not hold your hand until Tuesday the time is so long & my hand so useless. Adieu my delight."[24]

In 1848, Taylor returned to London after traveling with Mill, only to discover that her husband had fallen gravely ill with cancer. For a period of two months, she dedicated herself entirely to caring for him and saw Mill not at all, restricting herself to correspondence, some of it angry, even bitter, and full of dignity: "You talk of my writing to you 'at some odd time when a change of subject of thought may be rather a relief than otherwise'! *odd time!* indeed you must be ignorant profoundly of all that *friendship* or *anxiety* means when you can use such pitiful narrow hearted expressions."[25]

And as her husband neared the end: "The sadness & horror of Nature's daily doings exceed a million fold all the attempts of Poets! There is nothing on earth I would not do for him & there is nothing on earth which *can* be done. Do not write."[26] (Those who read Taylor's letters might be excused for falling a little in love with her.)

In 1851, two years after her husband's death, she and Mill were married. The event must have been joyful, a kind of completion, but as Hayek reports, "the marriage led to the most painful episode in Mill's life, his complete break with his mother and her other children."[27] The occasion for the break is yet another mystery. It must have had something to do with his reaction to their disapproval or their sense of scandal. But who knows? Hayek describes it as "almost as unintelligible to his relations as to us."[28] Twenty years after the break, his sister Harriet expressed genuine bafflement, reporting that "up to the time of his marriage he had been everything to us," and "it was a frightful blow to lose him at once and for ever, without [one] word of explanation,—only in evident anger."[29] Anger at what, exactly?

The marriage itself was quiet, productive, and supremely happy, but both husband and wife suffered from a series of illnesses. In 1854, Mill believed himself to be gravely sick. He wrote: "The only change I find in myself from a near view of probable death is that it makes me instinctively conservative. It makes me feel, not as I am accustomed—oh, for something better!—but oh, that we could be going on as we were before. Oh, that those I love could be spared the shock of a great change!"[30] But he recovered well, and it was Taylor who became desperately ill four years later. Mill wrote an appeal to a doctor: "I implore to you come immediately. I need hardly say that any expense whatever will not count for a feather in the balance."[31] He never came (perhaps because the letter arrived too late).

Shortly after her death, Mill wrote: "It is doubtful if I shall ever be fit for anything public or private, again. The spring of my life is broken. But I shall best fulfil her wishes by not giving up the attempt to do something useful."[32] *On Liberty* was published in 1859 and dedicated "to the beloved and deplored memory of her who was the inspirer, and in part the author, of all that is best in my writings."[33] Mill lived to 1873, and many of his greatest works appeared after Taylor's death.

Remarkably, Hayek ends his book saying very little about Taylor's influence on Mill's thought. But in fragments of the book, and in other essays he wrote, we can uncover Hayek's views on the mysteries with which he began. Hayek agrees that Taylor's "influence on his thought and outlook, whatever her capacities may have been, were quite as great as Mill asserts."[34] At the same time, Hayek concludes, "they acted in a way somewhat different from what is commonly believed. Far from it having been the sentimental it was the rationalist element in Mill's thought which was strengthened by her influence."[35]

It is important to see that for Hayek and his preferred version of liberalism, this is anything but praise. Actually, it is the opposite. In Hayek's view, there is an enduring opposition between true individualism, fundamental to liberalism as he saw it, and rationalism, which he associated with socialism and illiberalism (and also fascism and communism). By *rationalism*, Hayek meant to refer to the hubristic view that with the aid of reason, human beings can plan a social order, subjecting it "to the control of individual human reason," rather than relying on free markets, spontaneous orders, and the working of the invisible hand as described by Scottish Enlightenment thinkers such as Adam Smith, a founding individualist.[36] Rationalists, in Hayek's account, end up as collectivists, perhaps as fascists or communists. They foolishly think that human beings can effectively design rules and institutions, a "fatal conceit" that "always tends to develop into the opposite of individualism, namely, socialism or collectivism."[37] This fatal conceit leads to illiberalism, and to an obliteration of free markets.

Still, Hayek did not believe in complete laissez-faire. He favored a guaranteed minimum for the poor ("some minimum of food, shelter, and clothing, sufficient to preserve health and the capacity to work, can be assured to everybody"[38]) and even a comprehensive system of social insurance. His own conception of liberalism allowed all that (more on this in chapter 6). Nonetheless, he insisted that rationalism is both arrogant and dangerous, and he believed that Taylor moved Mill in its (illiberal) direction.

That is bunk. In my view, Hayek was obtuse in his conclusions about Taylor's influence on Mill. To be sure, Mill cared deeply about social justice, and he came to embrace what he described as a form of socialism, above all because of the unfairness of "the present economic order of society."[39] But his complex writing on that topic should hardly be seen as an endorsement of centralized government planning. Mill was never a rationalist in Hayek's pejorative sense.

Where Taylor most influenced Mill was on topics that were not the subject of Hayek's main focus. Hayek missed all this. Mill's *The Subjection of Women* (largely ignored during his lifetime) was profoundly affected by Taylor's views as expressed in her 1851 essay, *The Enfranchisement of Women*.[40] Taylor sketched many of Mill's central arguments, and others that were more radical still, including an explanation of why married women should work outside the home: "A woman who contributes materially to the support of the family, cannot be treated in the same contemptuously tyrannical manner as one who, however she may toil as a domestic drudge, is a dependent on the man for subsistence."[41]

On Liberty is widely taken to be an argument for limited government, and so it is. But it is crucial to see that in contending that people may be restrained only to prevent "harm to others," Mill was calling for restrictions on social norms and conventions, not merely on government. Much of his attack was aimed at the oppressive quality of public opinion. Taylor herself had made similar arguments more than two decades earlier, and it is hard to mistake the connections among her youthful views, his own painful experiences in the 1840s, and his passionate arguments against the tyranny of custom. As we have seen, his particular case for liberty emphasized the immense importance of allowing experiments of living. In his view, "The worth of different modes of life should be proved practically, when any one thinks fit to try them. It is desirable, in short, that in things which do not primarily concern others, individuality should assert itself."[42] That idea is the beating heart of Mill's conception of liberalism.

Here we can find the sharpest of the divergences between two of the great figures in the liberal tradition. Hayek generally prized traditions and customs. Recall Mill's words: "Where, not the person's own character, but the traditions or customs of other people are the rule of conduct, there is wanting one of the principal ingredients of human happiness, and quite the chief ingredient of individual and social progress."[43] This is a timeless claim, to be sure. But it is also intensely autobiographical. Mill and Taylor embarked for many years on a kind of "experiment of living" that was designed to promote their own happiness despite being roundly condemned by "the traditions or customs of other people." But their individuality asserted itself. The worth of their different mode of life was proved practically.

All this leaves the mystery with which Hayek started: Who was Harriet Taylor? Hayek's own verdict was clear. She "was an unusual person. But the picture Mill has given us of her is throughout determined by his own character and tells us probably more of him than of her."[44] To Hayek, Mill was in the grip of a delusion. Thus Hayek's speculative conclusion: "Behind the hard shell of complete self-control and strictly rational behavior there was [in Mill] a core of a very soft and almost feminine sensitivity, a craving for a strong person on which he could lean, and on whom he could concentrate all his affection and admiration."[45]

Though fascinated by the scandal and the romance, Hayek rendered a cold verdict on Taylor herself. Perhaps he was right. But I prefer Mill's own: "She was the sole earthly delight of those who had the happiness to belong to her. . . . Were there but a few hearts and intellects like hers this earth would already become the hoped-for heaven."[46]

4 THE RULE OF LAW

Many people admire the rule of law, but the admiration masks very different conceptions of what the rule of law is, and of what it specifically entails. As the liberal tradition understands it, the rule of law is best taken to have seven characteristics.[1] All of them are connected with the traditional view, signaled by many representations of the goddess herself, that justice is *blindfolded*. This is a vivid and puzzling metaphor. The liberal solution to the puzzle lies in determining what the blindness of justice represents.

Of course, it is true that some of those who do not consider themselves to be liberals are willing to commit themselves to the rule of law; the basic idea long predated liberalism. As Martin Krygier puts it, the "rule of law is not a liberal invention," but it is "central to most if not all liberal reflections on the nature, requirements, temptations, pathologies, and consequences of the exercise of power in societies."[2] In liberal hands, the rule of law turns out to be connected with freedom, and with the idea of experiments of living, which it tends to make possible.

SEVEN CHARACTERISTICS

CLARITY AND GENERALITY

The rule of law requires rules that are *clear*, in the sense that people need not guess about their meaning, and that are *general*, in the sense that they apply to classes rather than particular people or groups. A unifying idea is one of *fair notice*. People are entitled to know what they can and cannot do.

Laws should be publicly accessible as well as clear and general. It follows that there is a prohibition on "secret law." Of course, excessively vague laws—banning, for example, "misconduct" or "excessive" or "unreasonable" behavior—are unacceptable, at least in the criminal context; they are akin to secret law in the sense that people are unlikely to know what they forbid. They can even be seen as forms of secret law. Compare the *rule of lenity*, followed in many nations, which provides that in the face of ambiguity, criminal statutes will be construed favorably to the criminal defendant. This principle is an outgrowth of the requirement that laws must be clear and not secret, so as to provide people with fair notice. The ban on bills of attainder—measures singling out particular people for punishment—is a traditional requirement of generality.

In the real world, some complexities arise on these counts, and liberals occasionally struggle with them. It is a fiction to say that would-be criminals generally consult the statute books in advance of their crimes. More fundamentally, we do not know the extent to which criminal statutes are understood by members of the general public. Undoubtedly, the answer varies from area to area, and in many cases people could not describe the law with much accuracy. (How much of the tax law do you understand?) Many laws, including criminal statutes, have a degree of ambiguity. No legal system can entirely eliminate official discretion to give content to law at points of application, which means that clarity and accessibility will be imperfect even in legal systems strongly committed to the rule of law. To some extent, this is a failure of the rule of law, but it is also a product of the limitations of human language and foresight.[3]

La Rochefoucauld said that "hypocrisy is the tribute that vice pays to virtue." The commitment to clarity and transparency does not count as hypocrisy, but in any legal system, achieving those things is a work in progress. Liberals are determined to do that work.

PROSPECTIVITY; NO RETROACTIVITY

A number of years ago, I taught for a few weeks in a country that is not (let us say) a liberal democracy. After a brief discussion of the rule of law in class, one of my students said, "In my country, what is not expressly permitted might be forbidden." He said it with a touch of humor, but also with horror, and more than a little fear.

In liberal societies, what is not expressly forbidden is permitted. You cannot be punished for doing something that was not unlawful at the time that you did it. In liberal legal systems, retroactive lawmaking is disfavored, and it is banned altogether in the context of criminal prohibitions. The prohibition on ex post facto laws is the clearest prohibition on retroactivity. That prohibition is fundamental to the rule of law, and to the whole idea of liberty under law.

More modestly, U.S. law includes an interpretive principle to the effect that administrative agencies will generally be understood to lack the authority to apply their regulations retroactively.[4] If the legislature wants to authorize agencies to do that, it must do so unambiguously, and if it does so unambiguously, there may be an issue under the due process clause—at least if people are being required to pay penalties when they did not know, and could not reasonably anticipate, that their conduct would be declared to be unlawful.

CONFORMITY BETWEEN LAW ON THE BOOKS AND LAW IN THE WORLD

If there is little or no resemblance between enacted law and real law, the rule of law cannot exist. If the law does not operate in the books as it does in the world, the rule of law is compromised. If the real law is significantly different from the enacted law, generality, clarity, predictability, fair notice, and public accessibility are all sacrificed. People must be permitted to live in accordance with enacted law. In a liberal legal system, people must also have the ability to *monitor official conduct by testing it against enacted law.*

In many legal systems, of course, there is an occasional split between what the law says and what the law is, and sometimes the split can be severe. In all nations, including those that have liberal legal systems, the law on the books is not *identical* to the law in the world. The frequency of the phenomenon should not deflect attention from the fact that this is a failure of the rule of law, and it should be remedied.

HEARING RIGHTS AND DUE PROCESS OF LAW

The rule of law requires a right to a fair hearing when people are accused of wrongdoing. You cannot be put in jail, or otherwise punished, without such a hearing. You cannot be imprisoned just because some public official wants you to be imprisoned. Recall Bob Dylan's emphatically liberal words: "Even the president of the United States sometimes must have to stand naked." Even the president of the United States lacks the authority to deny people the right to some kind of hearing.

More specifically, liberal societies allow people to contest the government's claim that they have done something wrong—something that meets legal requirements for either the imposition of harm or the denial of benefits. People who are alleged to have committed a crime, or to have forfeited rights to social security benefits or a driver's license, are entitled to some forum in which they can claim that they have not, in fact, violated the legal standards.

Ordinarily, the main purpose of such a hearing is to ensure that the facts have been accurately found. But there is also a point here about individual dignity. People should be treated as ends, not means, and it is respectful of their dignity to allow them to have their say.

There should also be some form of review by independent officials, usually judges entitled to a degree of independence from political pressures. Of course, reasonable people can dispute the nature and extent of the hearing and the process of review. If people's liberty is at stake, they deserve a full hearing. Judge Henry Friendly, a great liberal, offered the following ingredients:

1. An unbiased judge or tribunal
2. Advance notice of the charge and the grounds for it
3. An opportunity to argue why the proposed action should not be taken
4. The right to call witnesses
5. The right to know the evidence against one
6. The right to have the decision based only on the evidence presented
7. The right to have a lawyer
8. The right to have a record made
9. The right to a statement of reasons
10. The right to public attendance
11. The right to judicial review[5]

To be sure, the rule of law does not always require all of these rights. As the seriousness of the potential deprivation grows, the need for all of the items on the list increases. If someone is at risk of life imprisonment, she should have each and every one of these rights. But if a young child is being suspended from school, it is not at all clear that he has a right to a lawyer or to judicial review. And as the likelihood of an inaccurate outcome diminishes, it becomes less necessary to insist on extensive procedural safeguards.

If the government uses an algorithm that is pretty well guaranteed to be accurate, a reduced hearing might well be in order.

SEPARATION BETWEEN (1) LAWMAKING AND LAW ENFORCEMENT AND (2) INTERPRETATION OF THE LAW

Many kinds of institutional designs can be compatible with the rule of law, but liberals believe that it is exceedingly important to ensure that the people who make the law, and who enforce the law, are not the same as the people who interpret the law. Legislators ought not to be allowed to decide what their laws mean. Their job is to make the law, not to interpret it. Law enforcement officers are not supposed to decide what the law is. If they are allowed to do that, liberty is at grave risk: an eager or zealous prosecutor, or one with some kind of personal or political agenda, might push the law in his preferred direction. In general, criminal laws are supposed to be clear enough that police officers do not effectively have the authority to decide what counts as a crime.

These are points about the importance of an independent judiciary, separate from legislative and executive officials. It is true that in world history, many nations have not insisted on an independent judiciary, and have allowed judicial and executive functions to be combined. It is also true that we might have long debates over what an "independent judiciary" is, exactly. But the basic point should be plain: in the liberal view, the task of adjudication must be separate from the task of making or enforcing the law.

NO UNDULY RAPID CHANGES IN THE CONTENT OF LAW

Liberals believe that if the law changes too quickly, the rule of law cannot exist. People will not be able to adapt their conduct to what is required. They cannot plan. They might be unable to avoid punishment. The problem of rapidly changing law was a prime impetus behind the adoption of the United States Constitution. Hence James Madison wrote: "The mutability of the laws of the States is found to be a serious evil. The injustice of them has been so frequent and so flagrant as to alarm the most steadfast friends of Republicanism. I am persuaded that I do not err in saying that the evils issuing from these sources contributed more to the uneasiness which produced the Convention, and prepared the public mind for a general reform, than those which accrued to our national character and interest from the inadequacy of the Confederation to its immediate objects."[6]

Most unfortunately, unstable law is part of the fabric of many legal systems. Tyrants change the law quickly and often. Fascism leads to unstable law. Even in liberal societies, regulatory law in particular changes very quickly, thus making it difficult for people to know what they are supposed to do. In extreme cases, rapid change should be counted as illiberal.

NO CONTRADICTIONS OR INCONSISTENCY IN THE LAW

If the law contains inconsistency or contradiction, it can be hard or even impossible to know what the rules are. People should not be placed under mutually incompatible obligations. Sometimes the law imposes conflicting obligations, again making it hard for people to know what they are supposed to do. These are important pathologies of modern law, and they exact a high toll on both liberty and prosperity. From the standpoint of the rule of law, they are exceedingly serious problems.

MISUNDERSTANDING THE RULE OF LAW

The ideas outlined here cast doubt on many actual and imaginable practices, and on many actual and imaginable legislative initiatives. They support liberal reforms. They require bans on retroactive law, on vague law, and on secret law. They help explain the prohibition on bills of attainder. They also call for liberal principles of interpretation, which favor the availability of judicial review, "prospective-only" legislation, and the rule of lenity for criminal law, giving defendants the benefit of the (fair) doubt.

But some people, including some liberals, go much further. They understand the rule of law much more broadly. For example, some liberals think that the requirements of the rule of law provide an important check on what they see as partisanship or selectivity insofar as these are reflected in law. In this view, the requirement of generality forbids law from imposing selective burdens. In this notion lies much of the debate over the meaning of impartiality and neutrality in law.

Let's start with the United States Constitution. An influential discussion appears in Justice Robert Jackson's concurring opinion in the *Railway Express* case.[7] New York City prohibited anyone from operating an "advertising vehicle" on the streets—that is, a vehicle that sells its exterior for advertising purposes. But the New York law exempted from the general prohibition the use of advertising on vehicles that are engaged in the ordinary business of the owner, and not used mainly or only for advertising.

Railway Express, a company operating nearly two thousand trucks for advertising purposes, challenged the New York law under the due process and equal protection clauses of the American Constitution. The Supreme Court upheld the law. The court emphasized that judges should defer to legislatures and noted that the local authorities might have believed that people who advertise their own wares on trucks do not present the same traffic problems as do people in the business of advertising. The court added that "the fact that New York City sees fit to eliminate from traffic this kind of distraction but does not touch what may be even greater ones in a different category, such as the vivid displays on Times Square, is immaterial. It is no requirement of equal protection that all evils of the same genus be eradicated or none at all."[8] In this way, the court rejected the idea that the principle of generality imposed serious limits on legislative classifications.

Justice Jackson saw things differently. He took this seemingly mundane case as an occasion for celebrating the use of the equal protection clause as a guarantor of the rule of law—understood as a ban on selectivity. The equal protection clause, requiring the rule of law, "means that the prohibition or regulation must have a broader impact."[9] The requirement of breadth in turn serves a democratic function:

> There is no more effective practical guaranty against arbitrary or unreasonable government than to require that the principles of law which officials would impose upon a minority must be imposed generally. Conversely, nothing opens the door to arbitrary action so effectively as to allow those officials to pick and choose only a few to whom they will apply legislation and thus to escape the political retribution that might be visited upon them if larger numbers were affected. Courts can take no better step to assure that laws will be just than to require that laws be equal in operation.[10]

There is much good sense here. As we saw in chapter 1, a liberal system ought to require public-regarding justifications for the denial of benefits or the imposition of burdens. In a deliberative democracy, interest group pressures or legislative self-interest are an inadequate basis for law. The idea of deliberative democracy is of course separate from that of the rule of law. Nonetheless, the requirement of generality can bring into effect political checks that would otherwise be too weak to prevent oppressive legislation from going forward. Consider a law requiring people of a certain religion or nationality to go through onerous procedures before obtaining building permits or drivers' licenses. If the procedural requirements were imposed generally, they might not be imposed at all. And if such laws were imposed on everyone, and can survive the political process notwithstanding that fact, we probably have a guarantee that they are not so oppressive after all. In short, per Justice Jackson's argument: *Increasing the generality of a burden by vindicating the principle of equal treatment is a barrier to arbitrary action, because it increases the likelihood of political retribution.*

But here is the problem: How are we to know whether a seemingly narrow enactment must be applied generally? Many laws are less general than they might be, and because their relative narrowness is justified, they need not be extended more generally. Children cannot vote; electric cars are not subject to certain pollution controls; labor unions are exempted from antitrust laws. Are these forms of selectivity unacceptable? Is it illegitimate to say that blind people cannot receive drivers' licenses?

To know whether generality is required, we have to know whether there are relevant similarities and relevant differences between those burdened and those not burdened by legislation. The rule of law cannot answer that question. No one thinks that "generality" should be required when there are relevant differences. No one supposes that the speed limit laws are unacceptable if they do not apply to police officers and ambulance drivers operating within the course of their official duties.

Any requirement of equal treatment depends on a set of principles establishing whether there are relevant differences between the cases to which a law is applied and the cases to which it is not. By itself, the idea of the rule of law cannot supply those principles. If a law says that in order to receive federal employment, everyone who is not white must fill out extra forms and take extra tests, then we can easily see that the grounds for the distinction are illegitimate. If a law says that women must take strength tests to be police officers, but that men need not, we can conclude that there is insufficient generality in the law. The reason is not the rule of law. The reason is a principle of equality.

But sometimes selectivity is entirely legitimate, and liberals have no objection to it. If a law says that people who earn more than a specified amount of money cannot receive welfare benefits, there is no violation of the requirement of equal treatment. When we ask whether selectivity is permissible, we cannot rely solely on ideas about rules and the rule of law. We must make judgments about the principles that justify distinguishing among groups of people. We are not merely requiring generality, but asking who is relevantly similar to whom. The rule of law does not have the resources to resolve the resulting debates.[11]

FREE MARKET LIBERALISM

These points provide reason to question some prominent ideas about the rule of law and what it entails. Consider, for example, Hayek's influential discussion.[12] We have seen that Hayek was the twentieth century's greatest critic of socialism, and one of its greatest liberals. He also had a lot to say about the rule of law and what he saw as its association with freedom and free markets. With respect to markets, Hayek emphasized that information is widely dispersed in society, and that even if government planners are well-motivated, they cannot possibly have the information that individuals have.[13] In Hayek's account, the price system is a "marvel," because it encodes so much information—the information held by the countless people who decide whether to purchase, or not to purchase, goods and services. Hayek's arguments about the dispersed nature of information in society have enduring importance; they raise serious questions about some forms of current regulation, which fail because officials do not know what society knows.[14]

More on this in chapter 6. Let us focus here on Hayek's closely related argument about the rule of law, which he identified with an idea of *impartiality*. In his account, its antonym is a system of *planning*, in which the state picks particular winners and losers. Because the rule of law does not do that, it does not play favorites, and in this sense it is impartial. In the abstract, that sounds plausible. But what does the requirement of generality forbid? Hayek does not disapprove of all that is done in the name of the regulatory state. Government provision of public services is in his view unobjectionable. Nor does he disapprove of maximum hour laws, laws banning dangerous products, and laws protecting against dangerous conditions in the workplace. (Again, more on this in chapter 6.)

What, then, is prohibited? Hayek is concerned about those measures that "involve arbitrary discrimination between persons."[15] This category includes most importantly "decisions as to who is to be allowed to provide different services or commodities, at what prices or in what quantities—in other words, measures designed to control the access to different trades and occupations, the terms of sale, and the amounts to be produced or sold."[16]

(We should be able to see here that Hayek's focus really was on socialism.) But how do we know whether these decisions, or any others, are arbitrary? Certainly it is not impermissible for the state to require taxi drivers to show that they have good (enough) eyesight, or to ban people from practicing medicine without meeting certain requirements of medical competence. It therefore emerges that the state is banned from imposing qualifications *only when they are arbitrary on their merits*. But to decide this question, we need a theory of appropriate qualifications.

The problem is that the rule of law, standing by itself, does not and cannot supply that theory. The objection to Jackson's account of equal treatment applies to Hayek's account of the rule of law as well. He understood the rule of law to ban arbitrariness, which is fine, but we need some principles to tell us what is arbitrary, and the rule of law, by itself, is unable to do that.

What about price controls? So long as the prices are clear, transparent, and stable, controls are consistent with the rule of law (which is not at all to say that they are good policy; they usually aren't). Hayek thinks that since they abandon the touchstone of supply and demand, any governmentally fixed prices "will not be the same for all sellers" and that they will "discriminate between persons on essentially arbitrary grounds."[17] That might be true in practice, but in principle, we could easily imagine a fixed price for all sellers of cell phones, soap, and shoes. Of course, there is much to be said against government controls of prices and quantities, and much of what can be said against them relates to their rejection of the forces of supply and demand. But the judgment that price controls are "arbitrary" comes not from the rule of law, but from the idea that the appropriate prices and quantities of goods and services are set by the market. That is a reasonable judgment, but it is not part of the rule of law.

It might be tempting at this point to suggest that much of Hayek's discussion is simply confused, and that the rule of law has nothing to do with markets at all. This conclusion is mostly right, but too simple (and it is always hazardous to disagree with Hayek). There are at least three features shared by the rule of law and free markets. First, the rule of law does not make after-the-fact adjustments. Rules operate prospectively. The same is true for markets. Second, there is a sense in which both rules and markets are "no respecter of persons." For advocates of the rule of law, government, like justice, should be "blind." Many liberals like that idea. Markets are similarly blind. Third, both rules and markets work against measures that impose inappropriate informational demands on government. Price-fixing is especially objectionable because it requires the government to do something that it lacks information to do well. The same argument can be invoked on behalf of (at least many) rules. By setting out rules of the road or requirements for the transfer of land, the government can appropriately allocate informational burdens between itself and others.

On the other hand, the metaphor of "blindness" should not be over-stated. All laws do, in a sense, pick winners and losers. Certainly this is true for maximum hour laws; it is also true for the provision of governmental services. And though free markets may not pick winners and losers, it is often quite predictable who will be favored and who will be disfavored under the ordinary rules of property, tort, and contract, which make markets possible. We know, for example, that people who lack talents and skills are unlikely to do well in a market system. In some ways, markets will promote equality of a certain kind, at least if people are free to enter them, and if they have a relevant background and ability to use them to their advantage (see chapter 8). Caste-like systems are defined by exclusion of identified groups of people from markets. That is a serious problem. But it does not have a great deal to do with the rule of law.

Could a system of planning comply with the rule of law, if the "plans" were announced in advance and if expectations were firmly protected? In a way, that question is the nub of the matter, at least for Hayek's largest claims. To answer it, we need to return to what the rule of law requires. We have already identified its essential ingredients, which include generality, clarity, transparency, nonretroactivity, application in the world as on the books, and hearing rights. As a strictly logical matter, a system of planning could indeed comply with all of these requirements. The price of certain goods could be announced for the next year, and so could wages. In that sense, there is no inconsistency between planning and the rule of law.

But Hayek's real concerns might be pragmatic and empirical, and might not involve logical necessity at all. Real-world systems of socialist-style planning might shift too rapidly to conform to the requirements of the rule of law. In addition, actual practice is highly likely to confound plans, ensuring that what happens in practice will not resemble what is said on the lawbooks. These points are part of the enduring argument against socialist systems. They also help explain Hayek's efforts to invoke the rule of law as an objection to planning. But he was wrong to conflate the rule of law with the commitment to free markets. He was a liberal, and a defining one, but there are other forms of liberalism, enthusiastic about the rule of law but less enthusiastic about the commitment to free markets.

These points raise questions about Hayek's view and also for the same reasons cast serious doubt on Marxist-inspired attacks on the rule of law. Recall Morton Horwitz's suggestion:

> I do not see how a Man of the Left can describe the rule of law as "an unqualified human good"! It undoubtedly restrains power, but it also prevents power's benevolent exercise. It creates formal equality—a not inconsiderable virtue—but it promotes substantive inequality by creating a consciousness that radically separates law from politics, means from ends, processes from outcomes. By promoting procedural justice it enables the shrewd, the calculating, and the wealthy to manipulate its forms to their own advantage. And it ratifies and legitimates an adversarial, competitive, and atomistic conception of human relations.[18]

This passage takes the rule of law to require much more than, in fact, it does. Does the rule of law forbid the pursuit of substantive equality through, for example, progressive income taxes, welfare and employment programs, antidiscrimination laws, and much more? Like Hayek, Horwitz appears to identify the rule of law with free markets. The identification is unwarranted.

A familiar challenge to rules—that they are connected with merely "formal" equality—is therefore off the mark. Rules could provide that no person may have more than one dollar more than anyone else, that the average income of men and women must be the same, or that all racial groups must have the same per capita wealth. There is no association between the rule of law on the one hand and economic inequality on the other. The rule of law is important, but we should not overstate what it entails.

WHY LIBERALS LIKE RULES

Now let us shift the focus a bit. Are rules good, simply because they are rules? That would be a preposterous proposition. Rules can be foolish or cruel. They can intrude on liberty; they can deny equal treatment. It is easy to imagine a rule that is inconsistent with every plausible conception of equality.

At the same time, rules have many virtues, and liberals celebrate them. Rules might produce incompletely theorized agreements, understood as agreements by people who disagree about fundamental values, or who are not sure what they think about fundamental values. They might do this in two different ways. First, people can agree that a rule is binding or authoritative, without agreeing on a theory of why it is binding, and without agreeing that the rule is good. That can be a terrific advantage, because it greatly simplifies life and prevents controversies from breaking out at the point of application. We can agree: "That is the rule, whether we like it or not." Theories of legitimate authority are varied and pluralistic, and acceptance of rules can proceed from diverse foundations.

Second, people can often judge that a certain rule is reasonable, without taking a stand on large issues of the right or the good. People can support a sixty-five-mile-per-hour speed limit, a prohibition on bringing elephants into restaurants, a ten-year minimum sentence for attempted rape, and much more without taking a stand on debates between Kantians and utilitarians, and without saying a word about their religious convictions. In these ways, rules sharply diminish the level of disagreement among people who are subject to them and among people who must interpret and apply them. When rules are in place, high-level theories need not be invoked for us to know what rules mean and whether they are binding.

Apart from their relationship to incompletely theorized agreements, liberals defend rules in multiple ways. What follows will be more a catalog than an argument. My hope is that the accumulation of points will help explain the enduring appeal of the rules and the rule of law.

1. *Rules minimize the informational and political costs of reaching decisions in particular cases.* Without rules, decisions can be extremely expensive to make; rules produce enormous efficiency gains. They can be seen as a kind of "second-order decision," chosen to eliminate the burdens associated with case-by-case decisions.[19] Presumptions and standards are also second-order decisions, but if we want to simplify judgments on the spot, and to try to make them mechanical, then rules are best. People understand that point and adopt rules—for example, automatic payment of credit card bills, or family dinner every Sunday night, or no texting while driving.

Every day we operate as we do because of rules, legal and non-legal, and often the rules are so internalized that they become second nature, greatly easing the costs of decisions and making it possible to devote our attention to other matters. With a speed limit law, for example, we do not have to decide how fast to drive. With rules, the complex and sometimes morally charged question of *what issues are relevant* itself has been decided in advance.

Rules are disabling for just this reason; they constrain us, but they are enabling, even liberating.[20] The point is easy to overlook, but like the rules of grammar, they help make social life possible. If we know that there will be one and only one president, then we do not have to decide how many presidents there will be. Constitutions are enabling for that reason, and the same point holds for many legal rules. If we know that a will must have two witnesses, we do not have to decide, in each case, how many witnesses a will must have. Rules both free up time for other matters and facilitate private and public decisions by establishing the frameworks within which they can be made.

By adopting rules, people can also overcome their own myopia, weakness of will, confusion, venality, or bias in individual cases. This holds true for individuals and societies alike. Societies and their representatives too may be subject to myopia, weakness of will, confusion, venality, or bias, and rules safeguard against all of these problems. Behavioral science has pointed to an assortment of departures from perfect rationality,[21] and behavioral biases beset legal systems as well as individuals and organizations. Rules often work to overcome those biases.

These ideas justify the general idea that rules should be *entrenched*, in the sense that they should apply even if their rationale does not. If we substitute for rules an investigation of whether their justification applies in each instance, we are engaging in a form of case-by-case decision-making, and it is easy to underestimate the costs of that way of proceeding. Officials may be pressed by the exigencies of a particular case to seek individualized justice, without seeing the expense, and risk of unfairness, of that goal. It is notable that in the 1960s and 1970s, American administrative agencies shifted dramatically from adjudication to rule-making, largely because of their understanding that through issuing rules, they could decide hundreds or even thousands of cases at once and thus eliminate the various expenses of case-by-case decisions.[22] That shift persists to the present day, and it has produced significant benefits.

Some of the costs of rulelessness, or of departures from rule-bound justice, are simply a matter of compiling information. To know whether a particular pilot is able to fly competently, we need to know a lot of details. But some of the costs are of a different character. They involve values and politics as well as facts. Suppose that we are deciding on ambient air quality standards for air pollutants that produce adverse health effects, or that we are thinking about when to go forward with projects that threaten endangered species, or that we are trying to decide how to reduce deaths on the highways. Information is important here, but it is also necessary for multiple people to reach closure on hard and even tragic matters. For this reason, there may be, for lawmakers, high political costs or great difficulty in producing a rule. But once a rule is in place, individual enforcement officials can bracket those matters and take the decision as a given.

The high costs—informational and political—of ruleless decisions are often not visible to those who are deciding whether to lay down rules in the first instance. The Supreme Court, for example, can see that rules will bind its members, perhaps unfortunately, in subsequent cases, and the court therefore might avoid rule-making in the interest of maintaining flexibility for the future. The court might so decide without easily seeing that the absence of rules will force litigants and lower courts to think hard, possibly for a generation or more, about the real content of the law. In this way, the court can internalize the benefits of flexibility while "exporting" to others the costs of rulelessness. So too can legislatures see that rules would contain major mistakes, or that they cannot be produced without large informational and political costs—without, perhaps, fully understanding that the absence of rules will force administrative agencies and private citizens to devote enormous effort to giving the law some concrete content.

2. *Rules are impersonal and blind; they promote equal treatment and reduce the likelihood of bias and arbitrariness.* Rules are associated with impartiality. Their impartiality is captured in the notion that justice is blindfolded. Rules are typically blind to many features of a case that might otherwise be relevant and that are relevant in some social contexts: religion, social class, good looks, height, sexual orientation, and so forth.

A comparative disadvantage of rule-free decisions is that they increase the risk that illegitimate considerations will influence decisions. The administrative law judge awarding disability benefits on the basis of factors or standards may well be affected by his feelings for a particular claimant, issues of race, his opinion of the social security program in general, or even his mood on the day of the decision. With rules, people who are similarly situated are more likely to be similarly treated. Rules can reduce both bias and sheer "noise."[23]

Many debates about constitutional doctrine are related to this claim. For a period, the law governing the First Amendment consisted not of rules but of a set of factors: the government interest, the value of the speech, and the likelihood of harm.[24] But over the decades, the court has shifted in the direction of *categorical balancing*, consisting of rules that determine how different forms of speech will be treated and also consisting of distinctions among different categories of restrictions on speech. For example, the law flatly prohibits any restriction on speech that discriminates on the basis of viewpoint (as in a prohibition on speech that opposes the current president). The categories are somewhat crude and may in particular cases produce inferior results to a more fine-grained approach. But the very existence of the categories usefully disciplines judges in sensitive and difficult free speech cases.

The claim that rules promote generality and equal treatment, and in that sense fairness, requires an important qualification. In one way, rules can *reduce* fairness. One reason is that rules suppress many differences among cases; they single out a particular feature of a range of cases and subsume all such cases under a single umbrella. In this sense, rules make irrelevant features of cases that might turn out, on reflection by people making particular judgments, to be relevant indeed.

Should everyone who has exceeded sixty-five miles per hour be treated the same way? Suppose that you were speeding because you were trying to get your child to the hospital, where she needed immediate medical treatment. Should everyone falling in a particular, unfortunate spot on a social security disability grid be denied benefits? Suppose that you are subsumed by the rule, but that in view of the particulars of your situation, you really cannot work, and so should get benefits. If equality requires the similarly situated to be treated similarly, the question is whether people are similarly situated, and rules do not permit a particularized and perhaps more accurate inquiry on that score. In this way, rules may actually fail to promote fairness as compared with rulelessness in the form of standards or some kind of case-by-case decision-making.[25]

3. *Rules serve appropriately both to embolden and to constrain decision-makers in particular cases.*[26] A special advantage of rules is that judges (and others) can be emboldened to enforce them even when the particular stakes and the particular political costs involved are high. Rules may provide the basis

for courageous decisions that might otherwise be difficult to reach and to legitimate. Liberals emphasize this point.

Suppose, for example, that the Supreme Court has set out the *Miranda* rules, and that everyone knows that they will be applied mechanically to every criminal defendant, even people who are accused of committing gruesome murders. If so, judges can refer to those rules, and in a sense hide behind them, even if the defendant is especially despised, and even if it is tempting to say that the rules should yield in a particular case. Or if the rule banning discrimination against viewpoints is well-entrenched in the law of free speech, judges can refer to that rule in invalidating laws banning flag-burning, even in the face of severe and otherwise irresistible public pressure. Or suppose that the ban on unreasonable searches and seizures is implemented through clear rules, forbidding law enforcement officials from intruding into people's homes (or from listening to their calls or reading their emails). If so, courts can invoke those rules, and insist on them, even if alleged subversives or even terrorists are involved.

The key advantage here (one that can be a disadvantage too) is that rules make it unnecessary and even illegitimate to return to first principles. If judges decided on the content of law at the point of (morally and politically charged) application, and if they had to go back to first principles, then they might not adhere to those principles at all when the stakes are high and the pressure is intense. This is the sense in which *rules create courage*. Of course, it is true that if the stakes are sufficiently high, and the pressure sufficiently intense, judges might qualify or abandon preexisting rules—for better or for worse. But if rules are in place, and if they are understood as such, then the likelihood of unjustified qualification or abandonment is a lot lower.

In one sense, rules reduce responsibility for particular cases by allowing the legal authority to claim that it is not his choice, but the choice of others who have laid down the rule. Officials can claim that the previous choice is not being made but simply followed. When the rule is ambiguous, this claim is fraudulent. But it is true when the rule is clear. In a system in which rules are binding and are seen to be binding, the law can usefully stiffen the judicial spine in cases in which this is a valuable guarantor of individual liberty against public attack.

4. *Rules promote predictability and planning for private actors, legislators, and others.* From the standpoint of people who are subject to official constraints,

it is especially important to know what the law is before the point of application. Within limits, it may be more important to know what the law is than to have a law of any particular kind. When cases are settled in advance, people are able to plan their affairs and to do so with knowledge of what government may and may not do. I worked in the Executive Office of the President from 2009 to 2012, helping to oversee regulation, and from the private sector, I heard this complaint as much as any other: *We do not know what you want us to do; please be clearer.*

In modern regulation, a pervasive problem is that members of regulated classes sometimes face ambiguous and conflicting guidelines, so that they do not know how to plan. Under a standard or a set of factors, neither the government nor affected citizens may know about their obligations. Return, by contrast, to the *Miranda* rules, instructing police officers how to deal with those charged with a crime. A special virtue of those rules is that they tell the police what must be done and therefore eliminate guessing-games that can be so destructive to planning. So too in the environmental area, where rules are often far better than the open-ended "reasonableness" inquiry characteristic of the common law.

5. *Rules increase visibility and accountability.* Liberals place a high premium on accountability. When rules are at work, it is clear who is responsible, and who is to be blamed if things go wrong. This is especially valuable when the rule-maker has a high degree of accountability and legitimacy. A large problem with a system based on standards or factors is that no one knows who is really responsible if, for example, the air stays dirty or the crime rate goes up. If the *Miranda* rules create a problem, the Supreme Court is obviously the problem. But if the court sets out no rules, but a test based on factors, and if that test produces mistakes of various sorts, then the court may escape the scrutiny it deserves. If Congress sets out clear rules in the Clean Air Act, and if things go very well or very badly, we know which institution deserves the credit or the blame. But if Congress sets out open-ended standards, and essentially tells the Environmental Protection Agency to do as it likes, then accountability is significantly reduced. Citizens have to do a fair bit of work to know whom to blame.

There is a closely related point: without rules, the exercise of discretion can be invisible, or at least far less visible. By contrast, rules allow the public to monitor compliance more easily. The question is relatively simple: *Did they follow the rules?*

6. *Rules avoid the humiliation of subjecting people to exercises of official discre-tion in their particular cases.* A special advantage of rules is that because of their fixity and generality, rules make it unnecessary for citizens to ask an official for permission to engage in certain conduct. *Rules turn citizens into right-holders*—a point of special importance in the liberal tradition. Discre-tion, standards, or factors make citizens into supplicants. Importantly, fac-tors and standards allow mercy in the form of relief from rigid rules. But rules have the comparative advantage of forbidding officials from being punitive, or unmoved, for irrelevant, cruel, or invidious reasons, by a par-ticular applicant's request.

Compare, for example, a mandatory retirement law for people over the age of seventy-five with a law permitting employers to discharge employees who, because of their age, are no longer able to perform their job adequately. If you are an employee, it is especially humiliating and stigmatizing to have employers decide whether you have been rendered incompetent by age. A rule avoids this inquiry altogether, and it might be favored for this reason even if it is both over- and underinclusive. True, it isn't exactly wonderful to be told that you have to retire because of your age, but if a rule deperson-alizes the situation, then it has significant advantages. Or consider a situ-ation in which officials can give out jobs at their discretion, as compared with one in which officials must hire and fire in accordance with rules laid down in advance. In the first system, applicants are in the humiliating posi-tion of asking for grace.

From all these considerations, we see that the case for rules can be very insistent, especially in a world in which officials and citizens cannot always be trusted, and in light of the enormous simplifying effects of rules for busy people with many things to do. At the point of application, rules reduce the costs of decision—often to zero, or close to it. If rules are good, they may also reduce the costs of error: those who make case-by-case decisions might end up blundering because they lack information or competence, because they do not have the right incentives, or because their motives are not pure. A point that is especially easy to overlook is that *rules, and the rule of law, reduce or even get rid of noise.*

This point might seem to be a bit abstruse, but it is connected with my general claims here. The rule of law is not all that liberalism has to offer, but it is fundamental to liberalism. Liberals know that a government might respect the rule of law while also violating liberty, properly understood.

Liberals also know that a government might respect the rule of law while also violating equality, properly understood. Liberals note that a nondemocratic government might respect the rule of law. We should separate the virtues of the rule of law from the virtues of other ideas and ideals.

But for liberals, these points should not be deflating. No less than fifty years ago or a hundred years ago, or fifty years from now or a hundred years from now, an insistence on the rule of law is very much in order.

5 FREEDOM OF SPEECH

Consider the following statements:

"The moon landing was faked."

"The sun goes around the earth."

"Donald Trump won the 2020 presidential election."

"Space aliens are among us."

"Pigs really can fly."

"The United States military carried out the 9/11 attacks."

"Dropped objects don't fall."

"Dogs are descended from coyotes."

Many people believe some of these statements. Let us stipulate that all of them are demonstrably false. Let us also stipulate that some of them might be *misinformation*, understood as not only false but *intentionally* false. Should they be protected as free speech? Should they be protected by a free speech principle?

To answer these questions, we need to ask an even more fundamental one: Why is speech protected at all?

Liberals do not agree about how to answer that question. Many liberals insist that the answer lies in democratic ideals.[1] In their view, there is an inextricable relationship between free speech and self-government. Free speech is the right to protect rights. This idea lies at the heart of many conceptions of liberalism. Consider the canonical words of Justice Louis Brandeis on that point:

Those who won our independence believed that the final end of the State was to make men free to develop their faculties, and that, in its government, the deliberative forces should prevail over the arbitrary. They valued liberty both as an end, and as a means. They believed liberty to be the secret of happiness, and courage to be the secret of liberty. They believed that freedom to think as you will and to speak as you think are means indispensable to the discovery and spread of political truth; that, without free speech and assembly, discussion would be futile; that, with them, discussion affords ordinarily adequate protection against the dissemination of noxious doctrine; that the greatest menace to freedom is an inert people; that public discussion is a political duty, and that this should be a fundamental principle of the American government. They recognized the risks to which all human institutions are subject. But they knew that order cannot be secured merely through fear of punishment for its infraction; that it is hazardous to discourage thought, hope and imagination; that fear breeds repression; that repression breeds hate; that hate menaces stable government; that the path of safety lies in the opportunity to discuss freely supposed grievances and proposed remedies, and that the fitting remedy for evil counsels is good ones.[2]

For people who embrace this view, many falsehoods, and many lies, are unprotected by the free speech principle because they have nothing to do with self-government. ("Elvis Presley is alive and living in Hawaii"; "I won the local golf tournament"; "My neighbor, Warren Crisp, killed his cat last night.")

Other liberals think that the free speech principle is about individual autonomy.[3] On that view, freedom of speech has intrinsic rather than instrumental value. Freedom of speech is connected with freedom of thought. It is part of what it means to be autonomous; it is not protected because of its consequences. If this is what we believe, we might well protect falsehoods, at least presumptively; it is a fair question whether we would protect lies.

In another view, also with firm roots in the liberal tradition, freedom of speech is protected because (as Oliver Wendell Holmes thought) the marketplace of ideas is the best way of discovering truth. As he put it: "When men have realized that time has upset many fighting faiths, they may come to believe even more than they believe the very foundations of their own conduct that the ultimate good desired is better reached by free trade in ideas—that the best test of truth is the power of the thought to get itself accepted in the competition of the market, and that truth is the only ground upon which their wishes safely can be carried out. That, at any rate, is the theory of our Constitution."[4]

If we embrace that distinctly liberal view, we might not be sure how to handle falsehoods and lies; there are arguments both ways. But on plausible assumptions, we might also adopt a (rebuttable!) presumption in favor of protecting falsehoods, and perhaps lies as well. After all, falsehoods can help us discover what is true. (Maybe.)

On another view, we protect freedom of speech because speech is the principal mechanism or vehicle by which we communicate or cooperate with one another.[5] Those who adopt this understanding might want to protect falsehoods, but not lies. As Seana Shiffrin puts it, "Deliberately insincere speech should not garner the same sort of respect because it does not participate, even at the fringe, in the same values as sincere or transparent speech."[6]

I do not aim here to choose among these competing understandings. I will focus more eclectically on why a liberal social order might refuse to allow regulation or censorship of falsehoods. Some of those arguments point to the relationship between free speech and self-rule ("We the People"); others invoke the marketplace of ideas; others speak of autonomy. In general, however, the arguments are utilitarian in spirit. They consist of objections to what the world would turn out to be like if we allowed regulation of falsehoods. An understanding of those objections tells us a great deal about the liberal commitment to freedom of speech more broadly.

OFFICIALS CANNOT BE TRUSTED

Liberals emphasize that if public officials are allowed to punish or censor what they characterize as false, they might end up punishing or censoring truth. The reason is that their own judgments may not be reliable. They might be foolish or ignorant. However confident, they might be wrong. Worst of all, their judgments are likely to be self-serving. If a president, a chancellor, or a prime minister tries to censor speech as "fake news," the real reason might not be that it is fake. The real reason might be that it casts them in a bad light. The truth police are often minions of an authoritarian, trying to keep hold on power. A more particular problem is *discretionary charging*: officials go after those lies and falsehoods that put them in a bad light and ignore or celebrate those that put them in a good light.

In defending the right to say what is false, Mill made this point gently, arguing that those who seek to suppress speech "of course deny its truth; but they are not infallible. . . . All silencing of discussion is an assumption of infallibility."[7] Actually, that is *too* gentle. To support Mill's point, we should make a distinction between innocent error on the one hand and authoritarianism, or something like it, on the other. Officials might want to suppress scientific findings, sincerely but wrongly believing that those findings are false and also harmful. When Galileo was persecuted for claiming that the earth goes around the sun, rather than vice versa, his persecutors were perfectly sincere; they were clear in their own minds that Galileo was wrong.

By contrast, authoritarian leaders, when censoring accurate accounts of what they have done, have no illusions about what actually happened. They want to suppress the truth. Some of the most interesting cases are mixed. A leader may believe that he is being victimized by fake news, but his belief may be motivated; he wants to believe that the story is untrue, and he succeeds in acquiring that belief. He tries to engage in censorship for that reason. And again he is concerned about a specific subclass of lies and falsehoods: those that put him in an unfavorable light, or that jeopardize his goals or threaten his power.

For a case in point, or a series of such cases, consider the official reaction to freedom of speech during the COVID-19 pandemic of 2020. More than twenty nations responded to the pandemic by limiting speech, often on the theory that the limitations were necessary to prevent the dissemination of falsehoods that would cost lives.[8] Nominally, the goal was to counteract an "infodemic" that aggravated the public health crisis, and in many cases, that was indeed the goal. But in some countries, the law went much further.

In Thailand, for example, Prime Minister Prayut Chan-o-cha issued an emergency decree, prohibiting publication of information that "may instigate fear amongst the people or is intended to distort information which misleads understanding of the emergency situation to the extent of affecting the security of state or public order or good morale of the people."[9] The law was extended to criticisms of the government's own performance. In the same vein, the government of Hungary enacted a law authorizing three-year prison sentences for anyone convicted of spreading falsehoods about the virus that are "alarming or agitating [to] a large group of people"—and allowing five-year sentences for anyone convicted of spreading a falsehood or "distorted truth" with harmful consequences for public health.[10]

The government of Bolivia issued its own emergency decree, allowing criminal penalties against "individuals who incite non-compliance with this decree or misinform or cause uncertainty to the population."[11] Causing "uncertainty" is a vague crime, and it is likely that laws of this sort would be used to attack dissenters. In such cases, official fallibility includes simple error on the part of officials, but it also points to self-interested motives.

On Mill's view, official fallibility is a sufficient reason to ensure that we protect what officials deem to be falsehoods—and that we allow public discussion and counterspeech to provide a corrective, if a corrective is what is needed. That argument has immense power. Human history suggests that when officials seek to punish or block falsehoods, their real concern is dissent, not falsehoods. In connection with the COVID-19 pandemic, an especially vivid example comes from China. Dr. Wenliang Li was a whistle-blower who drew attention to the danger. In 2020, he was disciplined for "spreading misinformation."[12] (He eventually died of the virus.) In general, the right reaction to Mill's emphasis on the "assumption of infallibility" is an enthusiastic nod of the head and a standing ovation.

Even so, we should emphasize that many liberal nations, including the United States, have long forbidden various kinds of falsehoods, including perjury,[13] false advertising ("this product will cure cancer"),[14] and commercial fraud.[15] People are not allowed to say that they are agents of the FBI unless they actually are.[16] People are not allowed to lie in their applications for federal employment. In these cases, Mill's argument has been rightly and thoroughly rejected. It is important to say that in such cases, there is usually demonstrable harm, and it makes sense to insist that false statements are protected unless (at a minimum) there is such harm, or at least a significant risk of that.

CHILLING TRUTH

A different reason to protect falsehoods has nothing to do with official fallibility. It is that allowing government to punish or censor what is false might deter people from saying what is true. Liberals stress this point.

Suppose that you are told that if you say something false, you will have to pay a significant fine. You might not speak at all. You might decide to steer well clear of the line, meaning that you will shut up about a range of things that are actually true. Or suppose a legislature enacts a new law, a Truth in Politics Act, making it a crime for a newspaper or magazine to publish any falsehood about a candidate for public office. Journalists would undoubtedly self-silence, even if what they have to say is both truthful and important.

As four justices of the United States Supreme Court put it in the court's emphatically liberal opinion in *United States v. Alvarez*: "Were the Court to hold that the interest in truthful discourse alone is sufficient to sustain a ban on speech, . . . it would give government a broad censorial power unprecedented in this Court's cases or in our constitutional tradition. The mere potential for the exercise of that power casts a chill, a chill the First Amendment cannot permit if free speech, thought, and discourse are to remain a foundation of our freedom."[17]

For all of us, the mere possibility of a criminal or civil proceeding might induce self-silencing. To be sure, this problem could be reduced if the legal system had a perfect technology for detecting falsehoods. In a science-fictional world (and perhaps it is coming), the law would be able to tell, for sure, whether a statement is true or false, and it would never punish truth. If so, people could be perfectly confident that so long as they told the truth, they could not be punished. We would also have a safeguard against official fallibility.

That would be an advance, but it would not be close to enough to protect freedom of speech. The reason is that people say, and should be allowed to say, many things of which they are not certain. We have *degrees of certainty*. We think that our favorite politician is not guilty of the latest charge against her, but we are not certain. We believe that the earth goes around the sun, but we are not entirely sure. We think that childhood vaccinations do not cause autism, and perhaps we are very confident of that, but we might feel a shadow of a doubt. For much of what we say, even in public, we might be 51 percent confident, 60 percent confident, 80 percent confident, or 95 percent confident.

Even journalists have different degrees of confidence, and different thresholds for having enough confidence to speak or write. If falsehoods were punishable, people might not speak out unless they are essentially certain—which would be a significant loss to speakers and to society as a whole. In the face of potential punishment, people might stay quiet, even when what they think is right. What kind of democracy, and what kind of society, insists that people shut up unless they *know* that they are right?

Justice Stephen Breyer may well have something like this point in mind in insisting that "laws restricting false statements about philosophy, religion, history, the social sciences, the arts, and the like raise [serious] concerns, and in many contexts have called for strict scrutiny."[18] Justice Alito rightly combined that point with Mill's concern about institutional fallibility:

> There are broad areas in which any attempt by the state to penalize purportedly false speech would present a grave and unacceptable danger of suppressing truthful speech. Laws restricting false statements about philosophy, religion, history, the social sciences, the arts, and other matters of public concern would present such a threat. The point is not that there is no such thing as truth or falsity in these areas or that the truth is always impossible to ascertain, but rather that it is perilous to permit the state to be the arbiter of truth.[19]

This is an important claim. We can fortify it by emphasizing that (true) information confers benefits on society as a whole, not merely on speakers. If someone discloses something that is true and important, many people will benefit. We protect speech in large part because of the countless citizens who gain if they can hear what other people have to say. Of course, we can question whether falsehoods help anyone (a point to which I will return)—but if suppressing them suppresses truth too, then we might tolerate a lot of falsehoods, not for the benefit of the speaker, but for the benefit of all of us. The point is nicely captured by Joseph Raz: "If I were to choose between living in a society which enjoys freedom of expression, but not having the right myself, or enjoying the right in a society which does not have it, I would have no hesitation in judging that my own personal interest is better served by the first option."[20]

When free speech principles are designed to protect against a chilling effect, speakers gain, of course. They don't have to be frightened of the authorities. That is important. But an even larger goal is to help unknown and unknowable others.

All that is right and important, but before considering a chilling effect to be decisive, let us fuss for a moment. Is a chilling effect really a sufficient reason to protect lies and other falsehoods? All of them? Why should a chilling effect be a trump card? No one thinks that the ban on perjury should be lifted because it also chills truthful testimony (though it undoubtedly does at least a little of that). It is a bit wild to think that a ban on false commercial advertisements should be lifted because it also chills truthful commercial advertising (though it undoubtedly does at least a little of that). If you tell people that they can't impersonate federal officers, you might chill some truth, but that's really not a big problem.

Or suppose that what is chilled contains a great deal of falsity and a small amount of truth: what is chilled is 98 percent false and 2 percent true. If so, it is hardly clear that a ban on falsity is unjustified. To know how to think about a chilling effect, we would need to know its size and also the harm produced by chilling truth, along with the benefit produced by chilling falsehoods. The fact that banning falsity chills truth is a relevant consideration, and it is often decisive. We should start with it. But it is not enough to justify the proposition that all false statements should be protected as free speech.

What is necessary, in short, is *optimal chill*—the right level of deterrence, considering what happens to both falsehoods and truths. If an approach chills a very large number of very damaging falsehoods and a small number of not-very-important truths, we should probably adopt it. Recognition of a chilling effect on truth is important, but it does not tell us how to get close to the point of optimal chill.

Liberals recognize this point, but insist on returning to fundamentals. If you punish falsehoods, you will deter truth. That is not a good reason never to punish falsehoods. But it is an excellent reason for government to tread lightly, and to allow people a lot of room to say things that turn out to be false.

LIVING TRUTHS

Suppose that government could be trusted; suppose too that any chilling effect on truth would be optimal, or modest, or inconsequential. If so, should we allow censorship of false statements of fact? That question raises this one: Do unquestionably false statements have social value? The United States Supreme Court has often said that they do not, but liberals believe that that's wrong. Put to one side the case of white lies ("you don't look fat in that outfit"), or lies that are necessary to prevent harm ("no one else is here," said the parent to the man standing in the living room with a gun). In some cases, false statements—about, say, World War II or climate change—are helpful to those of us who know what is true. They might even be essential to us, even if we are clear about the facts. A strong possibility, signaled by Mill and central to liberal thinking, is that false statements can improve our understanding:

However unwillingly a person who has a strong opinion may admit the possibility that his opinion may be false, he ought to be moved by the consideration that however true it may be, if it is not fully, frequently, and fearlessly discussed, it will be held as a dead dogma, not a living truth. . . . If the cultivation of the understanding consists in one thing more than in another, it is surely in learning the grounds of one's own opinions. . . . He who knows only his own side of the case, knows little of that. His reasons may be good, and no one may have been able to refute them. But if he is equally unable to refute the reasons on the opposite side; if he does not so much as know what they are, he has no ground for preferring either opinion.[21]

Surely it is better to hold a living truth than a dead dogma, and if people say something false (and horrible), our convictions about what is true might catch fire, in a good and productive way. Mill added a separate point, fundamental to the liberal tradition, which is that false statements can bring about "the clearer perception and livelier impression of truth, produced by its collision with error."[22] Mill's point holds for a large number of false statements. If people are told that the moon landing was faked or that the Holocaust never happened, they can learn more about the truth of these matters—but only if the statements are not censored. Consider a classroom. If students make mistakes, the discussion might well be improved. Falsehoods put a spotlight on truth. They give it life.

Mill's point is sufficient to suggest that falsity, by itself, should not be taken to be a *decisive* reason to allow punishment or censorship. But again, and in Mill's own spirit, it's worth fussing a little. Mill's argument is pretty abstract. For one thing, it may not apply to lies at all.[23] Mill's own concern was limited to cases in which people were saying what they actually thought. Suppose that a politician proclaims that he won the Congressional Medal of Honor when he did not. Should we say that the politician's lie helped people to discover a "living truth"? If someone impersonates a police officer, is it a good idea to force people to find out that he is doing that?[24] Should the impersonation be allowed, on the ground that it promotes learning?

Or suppose that someone falsely tells a federal investigator that an applicant for federal employment is a cocaine addict. Should the statement be allowed because the investigator can learn that the statement is false? As Shiffrin puts it, "It is difficult to extrapolate from the right of the sincere to attempt to persuade others of what they believe, to a right of the insincere to engage in deliberate misrepresentation."[25]

It is true that falsehoods can prompt people to think more and better. If someone lies about whether a medicine actually works, about American history, or about climate change, he can initiate a process of rethinking and learning. That process fits with Mill's argument. We can take this point to support the proposition that falsehoods should not be punished unless they create serious harm. But what if they do?

A fair question. Still, Mill was right to say that people can learn from false statements and that living truths are far better than dead dogmas. He was correct to emphasize that falsehoods keep people on their toes, and so keep truths alive.

LEARNING WHAT OTHERS THINK

There is a related point, not emphasized by Mill, but exceedingly important in liberal societies. When people hear falsehoods, they can learn more about what other people think, and why. If people find out that many of their fellow citizens believe that climate change is a hoax, that vaccines cause autism, that President Barack Obama was not born in the United States, or that the United States was responsible for the attacks of 9/11, they will learn something that it is important to know. *Pluralistic ignorance*, understood as ignorance about what other people actually think, can be a serious problem.[26]

If falsehoods can be spoken and written, then people will be better able to obtain a sense of the distribution of views within their society—of what others actually believe. That can be a large benefit. For one thing, it can give people a sense that their own views might not be quite right; it can crack a wall of certainty. Apart from that point, it can provide people with valuable information. If many of your fellow citizens believe that the earth is flat or that climate change is a hoax invented by the Chinese government, then you benefit from obtaining that knowledge.

Again, this is not a decisive argument in favor of allowing any and all falsehoods. It works best for false beliefs that are sincerely held; it is much harder to understand the argument as a reason to protect lies. The argument does not justify protection of perjury and false advertising. And even for sincerely held false beliefs, it is inadequate. The benefit of learning what others think might be outweighed by the cost of allowing falsehoods to spread. The only point is that it is an important benefit.

COUNTERSPEECH, NOT BANS

The final point is intensely pragmatic, and it lies at the heart of the liberal commitment to freedom of speech. Banning or punishing falsehoods might simply drive beliefs underground. They might not be exposed to the light. They can be fueled by the very fact that they are forbidden. If the goal is to reduce their power, then allowing falsehoods to have some oxygen, and forcing people to meet them with counterarguments, might be best.

A law might forbid denial of the Holocaust, as German law does, and in view of German history, such a law might be a reasonable idea. Holocaust denial might fuel anti-Semitism, and perhaps a prohibition reduces real risks. But in the abstract, we cannot rule out the possibility that from the standpoint of the very people who support that prohibition, freedom of speech would be better. One reason is that suppression of speech might intensify people's commitment to the very falsehoods that it contains. Another reason is that suppression might create a kind of forbidden fruit, broadening the appeal of those falsehoods. Yet another reason is that suppression might be taken as an attack on individual autonomy.

One more time: None of this means that falsehoods are always protected. Perjury is against the law, and so is fraud, and so is false commercial advertising.[27] But most of the time, liberals ask: Isn't it better to convince people, rather than to shut them up? That isn't a rhetorical question, not at all—but it's the right one to ask. Most of the time, the liberal answer is correct: *yes*.

6 FREE MARKETS AND THEIR LIMITS

In no system that could be rationally defended would the state just do nothing. An effective competitive system needs an intelligently designed and continuously adjusted legal framework as much as any other. Even the most essential prerequisite of its proper functioning, the prevention of fraud and deception (including exploitation of ignorance), provides a great and by no means yet fully accomplished object of legislative activity.

—Friedrich Hayek[1]

Why respect liberty? We have seen that liberals give diverse answers to that question. We have also seen that Hayek's distinctive account, associated with his enthusiasm for free markets, was rooted in his critique of socialism and centralized planning. He emphasized that however well-motivated, planners have far less knowledge than participants in markets do. Many of his central insights grew out of what he saw as the fatal problems with centralized government judgments about prices and quantities. Those problems were above all epistemic. Hayek's emphasis on those problems captures an enduring, and greatly contested, form of liberalism. We are going to spend considerable time with him here.

Some of Hayek's most important contributions to social thought are captured in his great (and short) 1945 essay, *The Use of Knowledge in Society*.[2] In that essay, Hayek claimed that the great advantage of prices is that they aggregate both the information and the tastes of numerous people, incorporating far more material than could possibly be assembled by any central planner, group, or board. Hayek emphasized the unshared nature of information—the "dispersed bits of incomplete and frequently con-tradictory knowledge which all the separate individuals possess."[3] That knowledge certainly includes facts about products, but it also includes preferences and tastes, and all of these are taken into account by a well-functioning market. Hayek stressed above all the "very important but unorganized knowledge which cannot possibly be called scientific in the sense of general rules: the knowledge of the particular circumstances of time and place."[4]

For Hayek, the key economic question is how to incorporate that unor-ganized and dispersed knowledge. No particular person or group can pos-sibly solve that problem. Central planners cannot have access to all of the knowledge held by diverse people. Taken as a whole, the knowledge held by those people is far greater than that held by even the wisest and most well-chosen group of experts. Hayek's central point is that the best solution often comes from the price system. His claim is that in a system in which knowledge of relevant facts is dispersed among many people, prices act as an astonishingly concise and accurate coordinating and signaling device. They incorporate that dispersed knowledge and in a sense also publicize it, because the price itself operates as a signal to all.

Even better, the price system has a wonderfully automatic quality, par-ticularly in its ability to respond quickly to changes. If fresh information shows that a product—a television, a car, a cell phone, a watch—does not always work, then people's demand for it will rapidly fall, and so too will the price. And when a commodity suddenly becomes scarcer, its users must respond to that fact. In Hayek's account, the market works remarkably well as a whole, not because any participant can see all its features, but because the relevant information is communicated to everyone through prices. Call this the classical liberal's argument for free markets; Hayek's argument has helped define that argument for many decades.

Hence Hayek claims that it "is more than a metaphor to describe the price system as a kind of machinery for registering changes, or a system of telecommunications which enables individual producers to watch merely the movement of a few pointers."[5] Hayek describes this process as a *mar-vel*, and adds that he has chosen that word on purpose so as "to shock the reader out of the complacency with which we often take the working of the mechanism for granted."[6] On Hayek's account, the price system is an extraordinary device for capturing collective intelligence, in part because it collects what everyone knows, and in part because it imposes the right incentives. Many liberals think Hayek got it essentially right.

THE STATE

It would be possible to agree with Hayek's arguments about planning and prices while also thinking that certain forms of regulation are not out of bounds. In fact, Hayek himself did not abhor all regulation as such. His form of liberalism insisted on a large role for the state.

Consider these words: "Probably nothing has done as much harm to the liberal cause as the wooden insistence of some liberals on some rough rules of thumb, above all the principle of laissez faire."[7] Hayek did not choose his words carelessly, and it is worth pausing over that claim. Or these: "To prohibit the use of certain poisonous substances or to require special precautions in their use, to limit working hours or to require certain sanitary arrangements, is fully compatible with the preservation of competition."[8] In Hayek's view, "The only question here is whether in the particular instance the advantages gained are greater than the social costs that they impose."[9]

Cost-benefit analysis is central to one form of liberalism (in fact, it is central to my preferred form, though many liberals do not love it[10]). Perhaps a mandatory seat belt law, a ban on trans fats, or regulation of exposure to certain carcinogens in the workplace would be unobjectionable. Do Hayek's arguments count against cigarette taxes, or taxes on sugar-sweetened beverages? Do they amount to a general large-scale objection to paternalism?

The answers to these questions are not entirely clear. In much of his work, Hayek was concerned with the largest and most abstract issues—the nature of liberty, the best conception of the rule of law, the proper role of government. On many specific issues, he did not offer particular prescriptions. Here is a revealing passage, written at a characteristically high level of generality, and worth quoting at length:

> There are, finally, undoubted fields where no legal arrangements can create the main condition on which the usefulness of the system of competition and private property depends: namely, that the owner benefits from all the useful services rendered by his property and suffers for all the damages caused to others by its use. Where, for example, it is impracticable to make the enjoyment of certain services dependent on the payment of a price, competition will not produce the services; and the price system becomes similarly ineffective when the damage caused to others by certain uses of property cannot be effectively charged to the owner of

that property. In all these instances there is a divergence between the items which enter into private calculation and those which affect social welfare; and, whenever this divergence becomes important, some method other than competition must have to be found to supply the services in question. Thus neither the provision of signposts on the road nor, in most circumstances, those of the roads themselves can be paid for by each individual user. Nor can certain harmful effects of deforestation, of some methods of farming, or of the smoke and noise of factories, be confined to the owner of the property in question or to those who are willing to submit to the damage for an agreed compensation. In such instances we must find some substitute for the regulation by the price mechanism. But the fact that we have to resort to the substitution of direct regulation by authority where the conditions for the proper working of competition cannot be created, does not prove that we should suppress competition where it can be made to function.[11]

From this passage, we can see that like most liberals, Hayek was keenly alert to the problem of externalities,[12] and that he favored "some substitute for regulation by the price mechanism." But he did not spend much time specifying his preferred "substitute."

Focused on coercion, Hayek showed little enthusiasm for paternalism, and while he did not discuss it as such, his work on liberty can easily be read to stand against it: "Coercion is evil precisely because it thus eliminates an individual as a thinking and valuing person and makes him a bare tool in the achievement of the ends of another."[13] This is a strikingly Kantian formulation, not speaking of welfare at all; notice the use of the word *evil* and the objection to treating people as means rather than ends. And indeed, Hayek seemed to embrace something like a Kantian, nonwelfarist foundation for freedom. "Some readers will perhaps be disturbed by the impression that I do not take the value of individual liberty as an indisputable ethical presupposition and that, in trying to demonstrate its value, I am possibly making the argument in its support a matter of expediency. That would be a misunderstanding."[14] Here Hayek does seem to align himself with Kant and to insist that liberty is an indisputable ethical presupposition, and not protected because it helps to promote utility or welfare.

But at certain points, Hayek extended his epistemic argument in favor of markets to make a very general claim, not at all rooted in "an indisputable ethical presupposition," on behalf of liberty and against coercion.[15] At those points, he emphasized welfare or utility, not Kantianism. Consider his suggestion that "the awareness of our irremediable ignorance of most of what is known to somebody [who is the chooser] is *the chief basis of the argument for liberty*. This is especially true in the economic field. If it appears that the market mechanism leads to the effective utilization of more knowledge than any directing agency can possess, this is the chief foundation of the case for economic freedom."[16] He put the point similarly elsewhere: "The case for individual freedom rests chiefly on the recognition of the inevitable ignorance of all of us concerning a great many of the factors on which the achievement of our ends and welfare depends."[17] This passage, emphasizing that planners (like all of us) know far too little, is in real tension with his endorsement of an "indisputable ethical presupposition." Different liberals take different sides on the right emphasis.

For Hayek, a key point involves that "irremediable ignorance," a problem that besets outsiders and planners. This can be taken to be a much broader argument than his claim that the price system is "a marvel." It captures a major strand in liberal thought, pointing to how little governments know. Consider this suggestion, also from Hayek: "If there were omniscient men, if we could know not only all that affects the attainment of our present wishes but also our future wants and desires, there would be little case for liberty."[18] It is worth pausing over that provocative statement. Hayek roots his claim for liberty, his most cherished ideal, in the absence of "omniscient men." If there were such men, we would be able to offer "little case for liberty." I disagree with that view, for multiple reasons, and I doubt that Hayek really believed it either; but let us not let that point detain us here.

Here, then, is where we are. Hayek defended free markets on the ground that they incorporate dispersed knowledge—far more knowledge than any planner, or any set of planners, can possibly have. His defense of free markets had a great deal in common with Burke's defense of traditions, and indeed, Hayek came to embrace traditions on broadly Burkean grounds. He also spoke of individual freedom as an end in itself, not a means. Free markets were, in his view, an essential way of protecting that form of freedom.

LIBERALISM, MEET BEHAVIORAL ECONOMICS

Hayek was keenly interested in human psychology. He wrote an ambitious book on the subject, where he emphasized that human beings did not have unmediated access to physical reality and instead saw it through categories of their own.[19] But nothing in his work in psychology presaged modern behavioral economics, and it would be a large stretch to say that Hayek was a behavioral economist in the contemporary sense. It would not be at all accurate to say that he anticipated modern behavioral findings.[20] Hayek did not explore the assortment of individual biases that have intrigued behavioral economists, such as *present bias* (a tendency to focus on the short-term), *optimistic bias* (a tendency to think things will turn out well), or *availability bias* (a tendency to assess risks by asking what comes readily to mind). Those biases have implications for how we think about liberalism and the whole idea of individual agency.[21] Suppose, for example, that people neglect the long term and endanger their own health and safety. What should governments do? Nothing? Should they let people die?

To be sure, Hayek was keenly alert to the fact that individual choosers lack important information, and that point played a defining role in his thinking. He often emphasized the extent to which each of us lives amid, and benefits from, a set of norms, cultural understandings, and institutions that were not designed by anyone, that have been built up over time, that serve essential functions, and that we do not and cannot understand: "What I want to show is that men are in their conduct *never* guided *exclusively* by their understanding of the causal connection between particular known means and certain desired ends, but always also by rules of conduct of which they are rarely aware, which they certainly have not consciously invented, and that to discern the function and significance of this is a difficult and only partially achieved task of scientific effort."[22] If there is a Hayekian theory of behavioral biases, it might begin there, and it might also emphasize that individuals might be prone to relying excessively on *local* information—that is, the information they happen to have by dint of local circumstance.

Hayek's frequent emphasis on individual ignorance is exceedingly important, and central to his thinking and thus to an important strand in liberal thought. But again, it should not be confused with contemporary behavioral economics—or with, for example, a suggestion that choosers may err when they decide whether to smoke or what to eat and drink, when they decide what health care plan is best, or when they select appliances or pension plans. When Hayek spoke of "irremediable ignorance," he was referring to planners and comparing them to choosers—an important liberal point that counts against paternalism, or any displacement of individual choices by outsiders. But as we shall soon see, behavioral economics puts some real pressure on Hayek's conclusions, and requires (in my view) a significant (but nonetheless liberal) rethinking of classically liberal approaches to markets.

MANDATES AND BANS

In emphasizing irremediable ignorance, Hayek sounded a lot like Mill, whose central arguments did not involve autonomy as such, but knowledge of relevant facts, and who was most likely to have it. Recall that in *On Liberty*, Mill insisted: "The only purpose for which power can be rightfully exercised over any member of a civilized community, against his will, is to prevent harm to others. His own good, either physical or moral, is not a sufficient warrant. He cannot rightfully be compelled to do or forbear because it will be better for him to do so, because it will make him happier, because, in the opinion of others, to do so would be wise, or even right."[23]

Mill's argument for his famous harm principle is also epistemic. Like Hayek, Mill believed that choosers are in the best position to know what is good for them. In Mill's view, the problem with outsiders, including government officials, is that they lack the necessary information. Mill insists that the individual "is the person most interested in his own well-being," and the "ordinary man or woman has means of knowledge immeasurably surpassing those that can be possessed by any one else."[24] When society seeks to overrule the individual's judgment, it does so on the basis of "general presumptions," and these "may be altogether wrong, and even if right, are as likely as not to be misapplied to individual cases."[25] If the goal is to ensure that people's lives go well, Mill concludes that the best solution is to allow people to find their own path, not least by learning from their own mistakes. This is a fundamental part of liberal enthusiasm for free markets.

So far as I am aware, Hayek never endorsed Mill's harm principle. Whether or not he thought that it was too weak or too stringent, his arguments against coercion, and Mill's overlapping defense of the harm principle, must contend with behavioral findings. Emphasizing the occasional human propensity to blunder, some people have been arguing that mandates and bans have a fresh justification.[26] Although offered by liberals like philosopher Sarah Conly,[27] those arguments seem profoundly anti-Hayekian because they support coercion. If coercive paternalism is involved, we might think that we are dealing with abridgements of liberty that are indefensible on Hayekian grounds.

But the motivation for coercive paternalism is clear: If we know that people's choices lead them in the wrong direction, why should we insist on freedom of choice? In the face of human errors, is it not odd, or even perverse, to insist on that form of freedom? Is it not especially odd to do so if we know that in many contexts, people choose wrongly, thus injuring their future selves? Many modern liberals press these questions. Recall, in this light, Hayek's words: "Coercion is evil precisely because it thus eliminates an individual as a thinking and valuing person and makes him a bare tool in the achievement of the ends of another." But those who defend compulsory seat belt laws, occupational safety and health laws, and mandatory saving for retirement do not think that they are making people into tools for the ends of others. They think that they are helping people to avoid serious and perhaps life-threatening errors. Why is that so bad?

No one doubts that in some cases, people lack relevant information; Hayek himself emphasized that point, not only in speaking of the dispersed nature of knowledge, but also in defending government information campaigns. Thus:

> Where . . . most individuals do not even know that there is useful knowledge available and worth paying for, it will often be an advantageous investment for the community to bear some of the costs of spreading such knowledge. We all have an interest in our fellow citizens' being put in a position to choose wisely, and if some have not yet awakened to the possibilities which technological developments offer, a comparatively small outlay may often be sufficient to induce the individuals to take advantage of new opportunities and thence to advance further on their own initiative.[28]

Is Hayek endorsing a kind of *nudging*, understanding that term to refer to interventions that preserve freedom of choice while also steering people in identifiable directions?[29] No doubt about it (if, as we should, we include educative nudges). In other cases, we can identify a *behavioral market failure*, in the sense that people fall prey to an identifiable behavioral bias (such as present bias), and their choices make their lives go worse by their own lights. When this is so, contemporary liberals might well put some kind of corrective response on the table, perhaps in the form of a nudge (understood as an intervention, such as a warning, that maintains freedom of choice), perhaps in the form of a tax, perhaps in the form of a mandate. To be sure, liberals would have a strong preference for a nudge, on the ground that it preserves liberty. If you want to eat high-calorie foods, nudges allow you to do that, and if you do not want to participate in some savings program, nudges allow you to opt out.

Notwithstanding Hayek and Mill, many liberals insist that some kind of planner, or choice architect, might have more information than choosers do, and might not fall prey to a behavioral bias. It is important, of course, to emphasize the word *might*. Liberals emphasize that planners might claim to find a behavioral bias when there is no such thing. Planners might have (bad) incentives of their own. Planners might be subject to the influence of well-organized private groups (an especially important liberal theme); planners might themselves be subject to behavioral biases. Still, a corrective response would seem to be on the table, even on liberal premises.

But putting a response, such as a nudge, on the table is one thing; deciding whether to impose it, and choosing its content, is another. Hayek did not speak to the question of how to proceed in the face of individual departures from perfect rationality. He did not argue, and did not believe, that departures from perfect rationality did not occur.[30] While he offered serious objections to planning, he did not explore such questions as whether salient disclosures of health risks are essential to overcome limited attention, whether automatic enrollment in a retirement plan is an appropriate response to inertia or procrastination, or whether fuel economy mandates are an appropriate response to present bias and myopic loss aversion. His high-level concerns about coercion, and about the deficiencies of planners, cannot resolve concrete questions of this kind.

LIBERAL BEHAVIORAL ECONOMICS

If there is such a thing as liberal behavioral economics, it would firmly reject the idea that public officials should be content to identify individual errors and declare victory. An approach with liberal foundations might engage in a comparative analysis: How costly are those errors, compared with the errors that would be introduced by corrective efforts? To engage in that analysis, one would have to know something about the relevant institutions. If a decision is made to proceed with some kind of remedy, a liberal approach, rooted in both Kantian and utilitarian thinking, might try to reduce the knowledge problem by asking not what planners like, but *what individual choosers actually do under epistemically favorable conditions*. Indeed, that should be the liberal question.

In fact, a stream of research is asking exactly that question.[31] In practice, it can be disciplined by asking five subsidiary questions:[32]

1. What do informed choosers choose?

2. What do active choosers choose? (If we focus on active choosers, we will protect against the possibility that outcomes are a product of inertia or procrastination.)

3. In circumstances in which people are free of (say) present bias or unrealistic optimism, what do they choose?

4. What do consistent choosers, unaffected by clearly irrelevant factors or "frames," choose?[33]

5. What do people choose when their viewscreen is broad, and they do not suffer from limited attention?

In principle, the best approach, and an emphatically liberal one, would be to ask all five questions. Active choosers who are uninformed might blunder; the same is true of informed choosers who procrastinate or suffer from inertia. If we learn what consistent, informed, and active choosers, uninfluenced by present bias or limited attention, choose, we might have real guidance (assuming that inconsistent, uninformed, and passive choosers, influenced by present bias or limited attention, are not otherwise differently situated from the former group). All of the questions can be answered empirically, and what we might call *liberal behavioral economics* is trying to do exactly that. For example:

1. A simple absence of information might lead consumers to fail to choose fuel-efficient motor vehicles, suggesting that some kind of nudge, or perhaps even a mandate, would be a good idea. Experiments might be designed to provide consumers with relevant information and see what they choose.[34] The choices of informed consumers might be taken as the foundation for analysis of the value of an intervention.

2. Suppose that most consumers make an active choice to enroll in certain programs, when those programs are designed so as to promote active choosing. If so, there is at least some reason to think that such programs are in consumers' interests. If most consumers do not enroll in such programs when active choosing is not promoted, then we have reason to think that their failure to do so might be a product of inertia or inattention.[35]

3. Experiments might be designed to make the potential economic savings of (say) energy-efficient appliances highly salient, at least potentially overcoming present bias and limited attention.[36] If consumers choose or do not choose energy-efficient appliances in such circumstances, we will have learned something about what is likely to increase their welfare— not everything, but something.

4. Should employers offer opt-in savings plans or opt-out plans? Suppose that many employees are affected by the frame; whether they end up in a savings plan depends on whether it is opt in or opt out. Suppose that many others are unaffected by the frame; they choose consistently. If the consistent choosers are not different from the inconsistent ones, except for the fact that they are affected by the frame, we have a reason to think that the choices of the consistent choosers are the right ones.[37]

5. When people are giving clarity about a wide range of product characteristics, we might investigate what they choose. Suppose, for example, that hidden fees are made clear and conspicuous so that people with limited attention can see them. What do people choose then?

Of course, there might be heterogeneity in the relevant population, making it challenging to generalize from what some part of a population does. But suppose that there is no such heterogeneity. In principle and sometimes in practice, efforts to answer these subsidiary questions should help with welfare analysis, where it is often challenging to know how to proceed when behavioral findings seem to cast doubt on standard uses of revealed preferences.[38] And, in fact, efforts to answer the subsidiary questions might justify some kind of response, not because planners like responses in the abstract, but because (liberal) planners are building on the choices of (the right) choosers.

WHAT IS TO BE DONE

No liberal believes that fines or subsidies are a sufficient approach to the problem of violent crime. No liberal thinks that people get to choose whether to steal or to assault. In the face of a standard market failure, government intervention has a familiar justification; consider the problem of air pollution. It is true that even in such contexts, default rules may have an important role; consider the possibility of automatic enrollment in clean energy.[39] But the effects of defaults, taken by themselves, might well prove too modest for the problem at hand, and they hardly exhaust the repertoire of appropriate responses.

In many contexts, including occupational safety, energy policy, anti-discrimination policy, and antipoverty policy, there are behavioral market failures as well.[40] If people are suffering from present bias, unrealistic optimism, limited attention, or a problem of self-control, and if the result is a serious welfare loss for those people, then there is a liberal argument for some kind of public response, potentially including mandates. When people are running high risks of mortality or otherwise ruining their lives, it might make sense to adopt a mandate or a ban, certainly on welfare grounds. (Admittedly, it is not at all clear that Hayek would agree; consider his sharp remarks about coercion.) After all, people have to get prescriptions for certain kinds of medicines, and even in freedom-loving societies, people are forbidden from buying certain foods, or running certain risks in the workplace, simply because the dangers are too high.

Whatever Hayek thought of particular restrictions along these lines, they were not his main target. Moreover, many occupational safety and health regulations must stand or fall on behavioral grounds; they forbid workers from facing certain risks, perhaps because unrealistic optimism or present bias might lead them to do so unwisely.[41] On liberal grounds, the best response might well be to provide information. But we could certainly identify cases in which the best approach, and an acceptably liberal one, is a mandate or a ban, because that response is preferable, from the standpoint of human welfare, to any alternative, including information, economic incentives, or defaults. It is also true, of course, that the right approach might be to do nothing—to allow market failures, including behavioral market failures, on the ground that the cure would be worse than the disease.

A LIBERAL CASE FOR FUEL ECONOMY MANDATES

I now turn to a case study, involving fuel economy mandates. I explore the possibility of defending such mandates, as opposed to economic incentives, by reference to behavioral market failures, captured in insufficient consumer attention to economic and time savings. The more general goal is to ask whether such mandates may reduce *internalities*, understood as the costs that choosers impose on their future selves.[42] I intend the issue of fuel economy mandates to be exemplary. A similar analysis might be made of cigarettes taxes, taxes on sugar-sweetened beverages,[43] savings policies, mask mandates, and many other problems. After sketching the argument in some detail, I will ask whether, on broadly liberal grounds, the argument might be found convincing.

Fuel economy mandates might simultaneously reduce internalities and externalities. On plausible assumptions, such mandates might even turn out to have higher net benefits than carbon taxes, because the former, unlike the latter, deliver large savings to consumers.[44] To say the least, this is not a conventional view, because fuel economy standards are a highly inefficient response to the externalities produced by motor vehicles, especially when compared to optimal corrective taxes.[45]

To be sure, everything turns on whether the plausible assumptions turn out to be true. What behavioral economists consider to be errors might be viewed, by some followers of Hayek, as not errors at all. My goal is not to run the numbers or to reach a final conclusion, but to make three more general points, which are (1) that mandates might turn out to be justified on welfare grounds, (2) that the standard economic preference for economic incentives misses something of considerable importance, and (3) that a liberal or even Hayekian approach allows us to make some progress in assessing points (1) and (2).

Gas-powered cars emit pollution, including greenhouse gases, and the use of gasoline increases national dependence on foreign oil. Recall Hayek's acknowledgement: "Nor can certain harmful effects of deforestation, or of some methods of farming, or of the smoke and noise of factories, be confined to the owner of the property in question or to those who are willing to submit to the damage for an agreed compensation. In such instances we must find some substitute for the regulation by the price mechanism."[46] With respect to greenhouse gases, we are dealing with something akin to "the smoke and noise of factories."

But what is the right substitute? On broadly liberal grounds, some kind of cap-and-trade system or corrective tax is the best response, designed to ensure that drivers internalize the social costs of their activity. The reason is that as compared to regulatory mandates, cap-and-trade systems and corrective taxes allow for competition and leave the private sector with a great deal of flexibility. People can find their own means to the chosen goal, which means that economic incentives of some kind, and not mandates, are the appropriate instrument.[47] They can compete over means, and competition is a terrific discovery procedure.[48] For any given reduction in pollution levels, incentives impose a lower cost.[49] The choice between a cap-and-trade system and carbon taxes raises a host of important questions, but they are not at issue here.[50]

For obvious reasons, a great deal of recent analysis has been focused on greenhouse gas emissions and how best to reduce them.[51] In principle, regulators have a host of options. They might create subsidies (say, for electric cars). They might use nudges (say, by providing information about greenhouse gas emissions on fuel economy labels).[52] They might impose regulatory mandates (say, with fuel economy and energy efficiency standards). Careful analysis suggests that carbon taxes can produce reductions in greenhouse gas emissions at a small fraction of the cost of fuel economy mandates.[53] By one account, "a fuel economy standard is shown to be at least six to fourteen times less cost effective than a price instrument (fuel tax) when targeting an identical reduction in cumulative gasoline use."[54]

These are points about how best to reduce externalities, and on liberal grounds, they seem decisive. But behaviorally informed regulators focus on consumer welfare, not only externalities. They are concerned about a different kind of market failure. They speculate that at the time of purchase, many consumers might not give sufficient attention to the costs of driving a car.[55] Even if they try, they might not have a sufficient understanding of those costs, because it is not simple to translate differences in miles per gallon (mpg) into economic and environmental consequences.[56] An obvious response, one preserving freedom of choice and in a liberal spirit, would be disclosure, in the form of a fuel economy label that would correct that kind of behavioral market failure. In principle, such a label, if behaviorally informed, should solve the problem as it avoids coercion. Consider Hayek's words on the latter topic, again sounding quite Kantian:

> By "coercion" we mean such control of the environment or circumstances of a person by another that, in order to avoid greater evil, he is forced to act not according to a plan of his own but to serve the ends of another. Except in the sense of choosing the lesser evil in a situation forced on him by another, he is unable either to use his own intelligence or knowledge or to follow his own aims and beliefs. Coercion is evil precisely because it thus eliminates an individual as a thinking and valuing person and makes him a bare tool in the achievement of the ends of another.[57]

Labels do not do that. They do not coerce, and they also do not discriminate (a particular problem for Hayek, who opposed "commands"). In short:
labels should be used to promote consumer welfare, by increasing the likelihood that consumers will make optimal choices, and corrective taxes
should be used to respond to externalities. This might even be seen as the
liberal approach to the problem.

This position has evident appeal, and it might be right. But it would be
possible to wonder whether a label will be sufficiently effective; this is an
empirical question, not resolvable in the abstract. Perhaps some or many
consumers will pay too little attention to the label and hence will not purchase cars that would save them a significant amount of money. And if
some or many consumers are genuinely inattentive to the costs of operating a vehicle (at the time of purchase), then it is possible that fuel economy
standards, with a level of stringency that would be difficult to defend on
standard economic grounds, might turn out to be justified.

In support of that argument, it would be useful to focus directly on two
kinds of consumer savings from fuel economy standards, involving internalities rather than externalities: money and time. In the United States, the
vast majority of the quantified benefits from recent fuel economy standards
come not from environmental improvements, but from money saved at the
pump; turned into monetary equivalents, the time savings are also significant.[58] On these points, the analyses from the Trump and Biden administra-
tions have not been radically different.

The problem is that on standard economic grounds, which modern liberals should be inclined to support, it is not at all clear that these consumer
benefits are entitled to count in the analysis, because they are purely private
savings and do not involve externalities in any way. In deciding which cars
to buy, consumers can certainly take account of the private savings from
fuel-efficient cars. If they chose not to buy such cars, it might be because
they do not value fuel efficiency as compared to other vehicle attributes
(such as safety, aesthetics, and performance). Why not let people choose
what they want? Where is the market failure?

If the problem lies in a lack of information, the standard economic prescription is the same as the behaviorally informed one: *fix the label and
provide that information so that consumers can easily understand it.* We can
understand this prescription in liberal terms as a plea for an educative
nudge, rather than a more aggressive kind of intervention. And indeed,

educative nudges are a key tool in the toolbox of the behaviorally informed policymaker. They might be seen as part of the same general program favored by those who prefer *boosts*, understood as efforts to inform and educate people so as to promote their own agency.[59]

We have seen, however, that even with the best fuel economy label in the world, consumers might turn out to be insufficiently attentive to the benefit of improved fuel economy at the time of purchase, not because they have made a rational judgment that it is outweighed by other factors, but simply because they focus on other variables, such as performance, size, and cost.[60] The problem may be one of insufficient attention.[61] A behavioral hunch, discussed below, is that automobile purchasers do not give adequate consideration to economic savings.[62] Apart from savings, there is the question of time: How many consumers think about time savings when they are deciding whether to buy a fuel-efficient vehicle?

Such questions raise a host of empirical issues. But if consumers are not paying enough attention to savings in terms of money and time, a suitably designed fuel economy mandate might well be justified, because it would produce an outcome akin to what would be produced by consumers who are at once informed and attentive. Energy efficiency requirements might be justified in similar terms, and indeed, the argument on their behalf might be stronger.[63] If the benefits of mandates greatly exceed their costs, and if there is no significant consumer welfare loss (in the form, for example, of reductions in safety, performance, or aesthetics), then the mandates would seem to serve to correct a behavioral market failure. And indeed, the U.S. government has so argued:

> The central conundrum has been referred to as the *energy paradox* in this setting (and in several others). In short, the problem is that consumers appear not to purchase products that are in their economic self-interest. There are strong theoretical reasons why this might be so:
>
> • Consumers might be myopic and hence undervalue the long-term benefits.
> • Consumers might lack information or a full appreciation of information even when it is presented.
> • Consumers might be especially averse to the short-term losses associated with the higher prices of energy-efficient products relative to the uncertain future fuel savings, even if the expected present value of those fuel savings exceeds the cost (the behavioral phenomenon of *loss aversion*).
> • Even if consumers have relevant knowledge, the benefits of energy-efficient vehicles might not be sufficiently salient to them at the time of purchase, and

the lack of salience might lead consumers to neglect an attribute that it would be in their economic interest to consider.

- In the case of vehicle fuel efficiency, and perhaps as a result of one or more of the foregoing factors, consumers may have relatively few choices to purchase vehicles with greater fuel economy once other characteristics, such as vehicle class, are chosen.[64]

Of course, liberals should be cautious about accepting a behavioral argument on behalf of mandates or bans. Hayek himself was skeptical about the reliance on the wisdom of experts: "One thing, in fact, which the work on this book has taught me is that our freedom is threatened in many fields because of the fact that we are much too ready to leave the decision to the expert or to accept too uncritically his opinion about a problem of which he knows intimately only one little aspect."[65] Behavioral biases have to be demonstrated, not simply asserted; as I have noted, important research suggests that consumers do pay a lot of attention to the benefits of fuel-efficient vehicles.[66] Some of that research finds that with changes in gas prices, consumers adjust their purchasing decisions, strongly suggesting that in choosing among vehicles, consumers are highly attentive to fuel economy.[67] Other research points in the same direction. It finds that when aggressive steps are taken to inform consumers of fuel economy, they do not choose different vehicles, which suggests that a lack of information, and perhaps a lack of salience, are not causal factors here.[68]

On the other hand, some evidence cuts the other way. A large-scale study of actual behavior finds that after a significant correction of an erroneously stated miles-per-gallon measure, consumers were relatively unresponsive.[69] As Gillingham et al. write, "Using the implied changes in willingness-to-pay, we find that consumers act myopically: consumers are indifferent between $1 in discounted fuel costs and 15–38 cents in the vehicle purchase price when discounting at 4%."[70] Puzzlingly, many consumers do not buy hybrid vehicles even in circumstances in which it would seem rational for them to do so.[71] According to the leading study, a significant number of consumers choose standard vehicles even when it would be in their economic interest to choose a hybrid vehicle, and even when it is difficult to identify some other feature of the standard vehicle that would justify their choosing it.

It is also possible to think that even if consumers are responsive to changes in gasoline prices, they are still myopic with respect to the choices of vehicles, such as electric cars, that have technological advances. Graham et al. put it crisply:

Consumers are more familiar with changes in fuel price than with changes in technology, since consumers experience fuel prices each time they refill their tank. Vehicle purchases are much less common in the consumer's experience, especially purchases that entail major changes to propulsion systems. Many consumers—excluding the limited pool of adventuresome "early adopters"—may be reticent to purchase vehicles at a premium price that are equipped with unfamiliar engines, transmissions, materials, or entirely new propulsion systems (e.g., hybrids or plug-in electric vehicles), even when such vehicles have attractive EPA fuel-economy ratings.[72]

More broadly, the government's numbers, finding no significant consumer welfare loss from fuel economy standards, are consistent with the suggestion that consumers are suffering from some kind of behavioral bias. At the same time, the government's numbers, projecting costs and benefits, might be wrong.[73] (Hayek would insist on this point.) Engineering estimates might overlook some losses that consumers will actually experience. No one doubts that consumers have highly diverse preferences with respect to vehicles, and fuel economy standards should be designed to preserve a wide space for freedom of choice. Appropriate standards ensure that such space is maintained. Economic incentives have big advantages on this count.

A major question, of course, is the size of the benefits from alternative approaches. If the consumer savings are very large, fuel economy standards are likely to have correspondingly large net benefits. To give a very rough, intuitive sense of how to think about the comparative question, let us suppose that the U.S. government imposed an optimal carbon tax. Simply for purposes of analysis, suppose that it is $200 per ton, understood to capture the social cost of carbon. Suppose that in relevant sectors, including transportation, a certain number of emitters decide to reduce their emissions, on the ground that the cost of reducing them is (on average) $Y, which is lower than $200. The net benefit of the carbon tax could be very high. But it is not necessarily higher than the net benefits of well-designed fuel economy standards.

What about Kantianism? Suppose that we do not care only about net benefits, and that we insist that as free agents worthy of respect, people should be free to choose, even if they do not choose wisely. Suppose we regard that as an indisputable ethical presupposition. If so, we might oppose fuel economy mandates except insofar as they are meant to reduce externalities. Internalities should not be allowed to count. The question is whether Kantian strictures really should apply in cases in which consumers lack information or are acting on the basis of some kind of behavioral bias. There is a strong argument that they should not, and that government responses do not treat people disrespectfully,[74] even if the presumption ought to be in favor of nudges rather than mandates. Reasonable liberals reasonably disagree on such questions.[75]

LIBERAL REGULATORS

With these qualifications, a liberal argument for fuel economy standards, made by reference to behavioral market failures and to internalities in particular, is at least plausible. In this context, nudges (in the form of an improved fuel economy label) and mandates (in the form of standards) might march hand in hand. It is true that if the goal is only to reduce externalities, a carbon tax is far better than a regulatory mandate. It is also true that for Hayekian reasons, the best approach to internalities should not be coercion but instead appropriate disclosure, designed to promote salience and to overcome limited attention. But with an understanding of behavioral findings, a regulatory approach, promoting consumer welfare as well as reducing externalities, might turn out to have higher net benefits than the standard economic remedy of corrective taxes and disclosure. That approach is certainly on the liberal table.

Everything turns on what the evidence shows, and on the particular numbers. But in principle, regulation of other features of motor vehicles could be also be justified in behavioral terms; certain safety equipment might not be sufficiently salient to consumers at the time of purchase, and some such equipment might fall in the category of experience goods. Credit markets can be analyzed similarly.[76] The broadest point is that while the liberal presumption in favor of freedom of choice makes a great deal of sense, it is only a presumption. It might be overcome, especially when it can be shown that behavioral biases are having significant negative effects.

How can that be done? Can it be done in a way that can fairly claim to be not only liberal but also Hayekian? In view of Hayek's skepticism about coercion and top-down expertise, the answer is not clear, but return to the five questions with which I began. At least in the first instance, and possibly in the last, behaviorally informed policy ought to be based not on the preferences and values of social planners, but on learning from the choices of informed and unbiased choosers. It might well turn out to be possible to identify those choices. Once we have done so, we might be on the road toward identifying appropriate interventions, whether they involve nudges, taxes, subsidies, or mandates.

Perhaps it would be extravagant to claim that those interventions, defended by reference to people's choices under epistemically favorable conditions, are Hayekian. But it may not be extravagant to say that they are in Hayek's general spirit and respectful of his most fundamental concerns. They can certainly be counted as liberal.

7 THE SECOND BILL OF RIGHTS

The alms given to a naked man in the street do not fulfil the obligations of the state, which owes to every citizen a certain subsistence, a proper nourishment, convenient clothing, and a kind of life not incompatible with health.
—Montesquieu[1]

I ask Congress to explore the means for implementing this economic bill of rights—for it is definitely the responsibility of the Congress to do so.
—Franklin Delano Roosevelt[2]

Those who denounce state intervention are the ones who most frequently and successfully invoke it. The cry of *laissez faire* mainly goes up from the ones who, if really "let alone," would instantly lose their wealth-absorbing power.
—Lester Ward[3]

Do liberals believe in social and economic rights? Which ones? Are they foreign to the liberal tradition, or central to it?

I am going to approach those questions by attending to an important but neglected part of the heritage of the United States: the idea of a Second Bill of Rights. In brief, the Second Bill attempts to protect both opportunity and security by creating rights to employment, adequate food and clothing, decent shelter, education, recreation, and medical care. The presidency of America's greatest leader, Franklin Delano Roosevelt, culminated in the idea of a Second Bill. The Second Bill represented Roosevelt's belief that the American Revolution was radically incomplete and that a new set of rights was necessary to finish it. The Second Bill should be seen as a part of the liberal tradition, though liberals disagree about whether it belongs there. I believe that under the best understanding of liberalism, the Second Bill does indeed belong. One of my goals in this chapter is to explain why. In the process, I will be challenging the distinction between *negative rights* and *positive rights*, notwithstanding the fact that many liberals insist on it.

The Second Bill was proposed in 1944 in a widely unknown speech that was, I believe, the greatest of the twentieth century. The origins of the basic idea can be traced to the earliest days of Roosevelt's New Deal, even to his first campaign for the presidency, where he urged "an economic declaration of rights," which entailed "a right to make a comfortable living."[4] There can be no doubt that the Second Bill was a direct product of America's experience with the desperation and misery of the Great Depression.

As a matter of history, rights are a product of wrongs, and after a period of massive unemployment and poverty, it seemed only natural to argue on behalf of a right to economic security. But the immediate impetus for the Second Bill came from a fusion of New Deal thinking in the early 1930s with the American response to World War II in the early 1940s, and with the general effort to broaden and reconceive liberalism in light of economic and political developments. The threat from Hitler and the Axis powers deepened the New Deal's commitment to "security" and strengthened the nation's appreciation of human vulnerability.

At the same time, the external threat deepened the need for a fresh understanding of America's defining commitments and of liberalism itself—an understanding that could have international as well as domestic appeal and that could serve as a beacon of hope, an example of what free societies and liberal governments offer their people. Liberalism was fortified by the contrast with fascism. It is well to keep that contrast in mind today; some antiliberals and postliberals have not sufficiently distanced themselves from it.

There is a direct link between the Second Bill and Roosevelt's famous speech of 1941, in which he proposed the *four freedoms*: freedom of speech, freedom of religion, freedom from want, and freedom from fear.[5] The four freedoms were not the work of any speechwriter; they were dictated by Roosevelt himself, who insisted, in direct response to the growing international crisis and over the opposition of a principal adviser, that these essential freedoms should exist "everywhere in the world."[6] The Second Bill of Rights was meant to ensure the realization of freedom from want—which, in Roosevelt's view, meant "economic understandings which will secure to every nation everywhere a healthy peacetime life for its inhabitants."[7] During World War II, Roosevelt and the nation saw an intimate connection between freedom from want and protection against external threats, captured in the notion of *freedom from fear*. In his words, "Freedom from fear is eternally linked with freedom from want."[8]

Roosevelt's emphasis on freedom should be underlined. He was a liberal. He was committed to free markets, free enterprise, and private ownership of property. He was not an egalitarian. While he insisted that the wealthiest members of society should bear a proportionately higher tax burden, he did not seek anything like economic equality. It was freedom, not equality, that motivated the Second Bill of Rights. Roosevelt contended that people who lived in "want" were not free. And he believed too that want was not inevitable. He saw it as a product of conscious social choices, which could be counteracted by well-functioning institutions directed by a new conception of rights. During World War II, Roosevelt internationalized that belief, urging that security required freedom everywhere in the world.

Although Roosevelt's Second Bill is not well-known within the United States,[9] it has had extraordinary influence internationally. It played a major role in the Universal Declaration of Human Rights, finalized in 1948 under the leadership of Eleanor Roosevelt and publicly endorsed by American officials at the time. The Universal Declaration includes social and economic guarantees that show the unmistakable influence of the Second Bill. And with its effect on the Universal Declaration, the Second Bill has influenced dozens of constitutions throughout the world. In one or another form, it can be found in countless political and legal documents. We might even call the Second Bill of Rights a leading American export.

We can go further. The United States continues to live, at least some of the time, under Roosevelt's constitutional vision—his conception of liberalism. A consensus underlies several of the rights he listed, including the right to education, the right to health care, the right to social security, and the right to be free from monopoly. When asked directly, most Americans support parts of the Second Bill. They even say that many of its provisions should be seen not as mere privileges but as rights to which each person is "entitled as a citizen." Some contemporary leaders are committed, in principle, to freedom from want. But in terms of actual policy, the public commitment is often partial and ambivalent, even grudging.

Some of the time, the United States seems to have embraced a confused and pernicious form of what some people see as *individualism*. This is an approach that endorses rights of private property and freedom of contract, and that respects political liberty, but claims to distrust "government intervention" and to insist that people must fend for themselves. This is a part of the liberal tradition; there is no doubt about it. But it was definitively rejected during the New Deal era, and it has no roots in America's founding period. Its only brief period of success came early in the twentieth century. Roosevelt himself pointed to the essential problem as early as 1932: the exercise of "property rights might so interfere with the rights of the individual that the government, without whose assistance the property rights could not exist, must intervene, not to destroy individualism but to protect it."[10]

Remarkably, the confusions that Roosevelt identified have had a rebirth since the early 1980s, in part because of the influence of powerful private groups. The result is a false and ahistorical picture of American culture and history both at home and abroad. That picture is not innocuous. America's self-image—our sense of ourselves—has a significant impact on what we actually do. We should not look at ourselves through a distorted mirror.

To make a long story short, the Second Bill was spurred by a recognition that the wealthy, at least as much as the poor, receive help from government and from the benefits that it bestows. Those of us who are doing well, and who have plenty of money and opportunities, owe a great deal to an active government that is willing and able to protect what we have. As Roosevelt stressed, property rights themselves depend on government. Freedom requires not merely national defense but also, among other things, a court system, an ample body of law to govern contracts and to prevent wrongs, and the police. To provide all these things, freedom requires taxation. Liberals have long been aware of this point. Once we appreciate it, we will find it impossible to complain about "government intervention" as such or to urge that our rights are best secured by getting government "off our backs." Those who insist they want "small government" want, and need, something very large. The same people who object to government intervention depend on it every day of every year.

JANUARY 11, 1944

On January 11, 1944, the United States was involved in its longest conflict since the Civil War. The war effort was going well. In a short period, the tide had turned sharply in favor of the Allies. Ultimate victory was no longer in serious doubt. The real question was the nature of the peace. At noon, America's optimistic, aging, self-assured, wheelchair-bound president, Franklin Delano Roosevelt, delivered the text of his State of the Union address to Congress. Because he was ill with a cold, Roosevelt did not make the customary trip to Capitol Hill to speak in person. Instead he spoke to the nation via radio—the first and only time a State of the Union address was also a fireside chat. Millions of Americans assembled by their radios that night to hear what Roosevelt had to say.

His speech wasn't elegant. It was messy, sprawling, unruly, a bit of a pastiche, and not at all literary. It was the opposite of Lincoln's tight, poetic, elegiac Gettysburg Address. But because of what it said, it has a strong claim to being the greatest speech of the twentieth century.

Immediately after the Japanese attack on Pearl Harbor, Roosevelt had promised an Allied victory. "No matter how long it may take us to overcome this premeditated invasion, the American people in their righteous might will win through to absolute victory. . . . With confidence in our armed forces—with the unbounding determination of our people—we will gain the inevitable triumph—so help us God."[11] He had often insisted that the ultimate outcome was assured. The always confident president's earliest projections for American military production—tens of thousands of planes, tanks, and antiaircraft guns, six million tons of merchant shipping— initially seemed staggering, outlandish, utterly unrealistic. To the many skeptics, including his own advisers, Roosevelt responded offhandedly, "Oh—the production people can do it, if they really try."[12] In a few years, his projections had been greatly exceeded.

Yet in the early days of 1944, with victory on the horizon, Roosevelt believed that difficult times lay ahead. Fearing national complacency, he devoted most of his speech to the war effort. He did so in a way that explicitly linked that effort to the New Deal and the other crisis the nation had surmounted under his leadership: the Great Depression.

Roosevelt began by emphasizing that that war was a shared endeavor in which the United States was simply one participant: "This Nation in the past two years has become an active partner in the world's greatest war against human slavery."[13] The war was in the process of being won. "But I do not think that any of us Americans can be content with mere survival."[14] After victory, the initial task was to prevent "another interim that leads to new disaster—that we shall not repeat the tragic errors of ostrich isolationism—that we shall not repeat the excesses of the wild twenties when the Nation went for a joy ride on a roller coaster which ended in a tragic crash."[15] This sentence immediately connected the war against tyranny with the effort to combat economic distress and uncertainty.

Hence "the one supreme objective for the future"—the objective for all nations—was captured "in one word: Security."[16] Roosevelt argued that the term "means not only physical security which provides safety from attacks by aggressors," but includes as well "economic security, social security, moral security."[17] All of the allies were concerned not merely with defeating Fascism but also with improved education, better opportunities, and improved living standards. Roosevelt insisted that "essential to peace is a decent standard of living for all individual men and women and children in all nations. Freedom from fear is eternally linked with freedom from want."[18] This is one conception of liberalism.

In connecting the two freedoms, he urged, first and foremost, that America could be free from fear only if the citizens of "all nations" were themselves free from want. External threats are often a product of extreme deprivation faced by those who make those threats. But Roosevelt also meant to remind the nation that citizens cannot be free from fear unless they have some protection against the most severe forms of want—that minimal security, coming from adequate education and decent opportunity, is itself a safeguard against fear.

Then Roosevelt turned to the problem of domestic selfishness and profit-mongering. Amid war, some groups were attempting to "make profits for themselves at the expense of their neighbors—profits in money or in terms of political or social preferment."[19] He deplored this "selfish agitation," asserting that "in this war, we have been compelled to learn how interdependent upon each other are all groups and sections of the population of America."[20] Here he laid special emphasis on the difficult position of people who depended on fixed incomes—teachers, clergy, police officers, widows and miners, old age pensioners, and others at risk from inflation. To ensure a fair and stable economy and to protect the war effort, he proposed a number of reforms, including a tax law "which will tax all unreasonable profits, both individual and corporate," and a "cost of food law" designed to protect consumers from prohibitively expensive necessities.[21]

Much more controversially, Roosevelt argued for a national service act. It was vaguely described, but he contended that it would prevent strikes and ensure that ordinary citizens, no less than soldiers, would contribute to victory in war. As for soldiers themselves, he insisted that legislation be enacted to permit them to vote. "It is the duty of the Congress to remove this unjustifiable discrimination against the men and women in our armed forces—and to do it as quickly as possible."[22]

At this stage, Roosevelt turned to purely domestic affairs. He began by pointing toward the postwar era: "It is our duty now to begin to lay the plans and determine the strategy for the winning of a lasting peace and the establishment of an American standard of living higher than ever before known."[23] He added that the nation "cannot be content, no matter how high that general standard of living may be, if some fraction of our people—whether it be one-third or one-fifth or one-tenth—is ill-fed, ill-clothed, ill-housed, and insecure."[24] Suddenly the speech became far more ambitious. Roosevelt looked back, and not entirely approvingly, to the framing of the Constitution. At its inception, the nation had grown "under the protection of certain inalienable political rights—among them the right of free speech, free press, free worship, trial by jury, freedom from unreasonable searches and seizures."[25]

But over time, these rights had proved inadequate. Unlike the Constitution's framers, "we have come to a clear realization of the fact that true individual freedom cannot exist without economic security and independence."[26] As Roosevelt saw it, "necessitous men are not free men,"[27] not least because those who are hungry and jobless "are the stuff of which dictatorships are made."[28] He echoed the words of Jefferson's Declaration of Independence, urging a kind of declaration of *interdependence*: "In our day these economic truths have become accepted as self-evident. We have accepted, so to speak, a second Bill of Rights under which a new basis of security and prosperity can be established for all—regardless of station, race, or creed."[29] It is worth pausing over the last five words. A decade before the constitutional assault on racial segregation and two decades before the enactment of a general civil rights law, Roosevelt insisted on an antidiscrimination principle. Then he listed the relevant rights:

1. The right to a useful and remunerative job in the industries or shops or farms or mines of the Nation;
2. The right to earn enough to provide adequate food and clothing and recreation;
3. The right of every farmer to raise and sell his products at a return which will give him and his family a decent living;

4. The right of every businessman, large and small, to trade in an atmosphere of freedom from unfair competition and domination by monopolies at home or abroad;

5. The right of every family to a decent home;

6. The right to adequate medical care and the opportunity to achieve and enjoy good health;

7. The right to adequate protection from the economic fears of old age, sickness, accident, and unemployment;

8. The right to a good education.[30]

Having cataloged these eight rights, Roosevelt immediately recalled the "one word" that captured the world's objective for the future. He argued that these "rights spell security"—and hence that the recognition of the Second Bill was continuous with the war effort.[31] "After this war is won," he said, "we must be prepared to move forward, in the implementation of these rights."[32] And there was a close connection between this implementation and the coming international order. "America's own rightful place in the world depends in large part upon how fully these and similar rights have been carried into practice for our citizens. For unless there is security here at home there cannot be lasting peace in the world."[33]

Roosevelt asked "the Congress to explore the means for implementing this economic bill of rights—for it is definitely the responsibility of the Congress to do so."[34] He observed that many of the relevant problems were then before congressional committees, and added that if "no adequate program of progress is evolved, I am certain that the Nation will be conscious of this fact."[35] And he made a special plea on behalf of the nation's "fighting men abroad—and their families at home," many of them far from privileged, who "expect such a program and have the right to insist on it."[36]

He closed by unifying the two disparate topics of his speech—indeed, the two disparate topics of his presidency: freedom from fear and freedom from want. "There are no two fronts for America in this war. There is only one front. There is one line of unity which extends from the hearts of the people at home to the men of the attacking forces in our farthest outposts."[37] In so saying, Roosevelt attempted at once to unify the nation—those at home and those abroad—and thus quell the "selfish agitation" with which he began. He also meant to suggest that security, his organizing theme, could be provided only if the movement for the Second Bill could be linked with the movement for defeating the Axis powers. This, then, was Roosevelt's conception of liberalism. It is closely connected with more philosophical and economic accounts, including those offered by John Rawls and (even) Milton Friedman, who supported a negative income tax.

TWO DOCTORS

Roosevelt's Second Bill of Rights speech was an effort to integrate the two "doctors" who had occupied his lengthy presidency. Once the Fascist threat became serious, Roosevelt's domestic programs were put on what he saw as temporary hold, to the great disappointment of many of his strongest supporters. Roosevelt explained the shift in emphasis in some informal remarks distinguishing between "Dr. New Deal" and "Dr. Win the War." After the attack on Pearl Harbor, he said, the strategies of the first doctor were ill-suited to the new task:

> How did the New Deal come into existence? It was because in 1932 there was an awfully sick patient called the United States. He was suffering from a grave internal disorder—he was awfully sick—he had all kinds of internal troubles. And they sent for a doctor. . . . But two years ago, after [the sick patient] had become pretty well, he had a very bad accident. . . . Two years ago on the 7th of December, he got into a pretty bad smash-up—broke his hip, broke his leg in two or three places, broke a wrist and an arm. Some people didn't even think he would live, for a while. Old Doc New Deal didn't know anything about broken legs and arms. He knew a great deal about internal medicine but nothing about this new kind of trouble. So he got his partner, who was an orthopedic surgeon, Dr. Win the War, to take care of this fellow. And the result is that the patient is back on his feet. He has given up his crutches. He has begun to strike back—on the offensive.[38]

The call for the Second Bill was an attempt to connect these two doctors—to suggest that they shared the single task of ensuring security. Of course, Roosevelt himself, a victim of life-threatening polio, was never able to give up his crutches or "get back on his feet" (and his metaphor here could not have been entirely coincidental). But in his Second Bill of Rights speech, he was able to take the initiative, both domestically and internationally. The link between Roosevelt's two doctors was understood by his listeners. After the speech, *Time* magazine reported, not approvingly, that "Dr. Win-the-War has apparently called into consultation Dr. Win-New-Rights. . . . Some druggists on Capitol Hill thought the handwriting on the prescription seemed strangely familiar—identical, in fact, with that of the late Dr. New Deal."[39]

The first concrete result of the Second Bill of Rights proposal was the GI Bill of Rights, which offered an array of housing, medical, educational, and training benefits to returning veterans.[40] The GI Bill was exceedingly important. Above all, it gave millions of veterans a chance to attend colleges and universities. "GI Bill beneficiaries," according to Stanford historian David Kennedy, "changed the face of higher education, dramatically raised the educational level and hence the productivity of the workforce, and in the process unimaginably altered their own lives."[41] The fate of returning soldiers was a large part of what motivated Roosevelt to attend to domestic issues during the war; he defended the Second Bill partly by reference to the legitimate expectations of those leaving the military for civilian life. But the GI Bill fell far short of what Roosevelt sought to provide.

The greatness of the Second Bill of Rights speech lies in the fact that it captured the extraordinary twentieth-century revolution in the liberal conception of rights in America and elsewhere. Hence Roosevelt's speech marked the utter collapse of the idea that freedom comes from an absence of government. It also identified enduring innovations in American government between 1933 and 1944—innovations that embodied the rise of the modern state. The basic themes of Roosevelt's speech have echoed throughout American political life to the present day. In some ways, he was correct to say that the nation has "accepted" such a bill. By 1944, many Americans were undoubtedly prepared to endorse it. Most Americans continue to do so today. But the acceptance has proved ambivalent, and it has come under pressure from thinkers and powerful private groups with an intense interest in burying or delegitimating the Second Bill—and in recovering the kind of thinking that immediately preceded Roosevelt's New Deal.

LIBERALISM AND THE MYTH OF LAISSEZ-FAIRE

In the summer of 1932, with the nation mired in the Depression, Franklin Delano Roosevelt was nominated for the presidency by the Democratic Convention in Chicago. He began by violating an established tradition. Throughout the nation's history, it had been the practice of presidential nominees to stay away from the convention and to accept the nomination only after formal notification, several weeks after the event itself. Roosevelt departed from precedent and flew from New York to Chicago to address the delegates in person. He began by urging that his action should be symbolic.

"Let it be from now on the task of our party to break foolish traditions."[42] (So much for Burke.)

Roosevelt's speech electrified the convention. His declared goal was to "drive out" the "specter of insecurity from our midst."[43] What, he asked, do Americans "want more than anything else?" His answer was simple: "work, with all the moral and spiritual values that go with it; and with work, a reasonable measure of security. . . . Work and security—these are more than words."[44] He complained of leaders who maintained that "economic laws—sacred, inviolable, unchangeable—cause panics which no one could prevent. . . . We must lay hold of the fact that economic laws are not made by nature. They are made by human beings."[45] Roosevelt ended with the promise that millions of hopeful Americans "cannot and shall not hope in vain. I pledge you, I pledge myself, to a new deal for the American people."[46]

The term *new deal* was not intended to signal anything especially important. Sam Rosenman, the adviser who penned those words, said, "I had not the slightest idea that" the phrase "would take hold the way it did, nor did the Governor when he read and revised what I had written. In fact, he attached no importance to the two monosyllables."[47] But to the surprise of all, including Roosevelt himself, they came to capture much of his presidency, which indeed involved a kind of reshuffling of the social cards. Writing six years later about the origin of the phrase, Roosevelt engaged in a bit of revisionist history: "The word 'Deal' implied that the government itself was going to use affirmative action to bring about its avowed objectives rather than stand by and hope that general economic laws alone would attain them. The word 'New' implied that a new order of things designed to benefit the great mass of our farmers, workers and business men would replace the old order of special privilege in a Nation which was completely and thoroughly disgusted with the existing dispensation."[48]

The Second Bill of Rights was a direct outgrowth of these ideas. To understand them, and to see how Roosevelt and his New Deal altered the American understanding of rights, we must focus on two developments. The first is conceptual; it involves a major reassessment of what really happens in a free market economy. The conceptual development amounted to an attack, liberal in nature, on the whole idea of laissez-faire—a suggestion that government and coercion are not opposed to human liberty but in fact are necessary to it. The second development is practical, involving the Great Depression and the nation's reaction to it. The two developments are closely linked. Standing by itself, a set of conceptual claims is most unlikely to move a nation. But the Great Depression helped to drive the conceptual lesson home. The new understanding of rights was a product of a new understanding of wrongs.

In a nutshell, the New Deal helped to vindicate a simple idea, central to a long-standing strand in liberal thought: No one really opposes government intervention. Even the people who most loudly denounce government interference depend on it every day. Their rights do not come from minimizing government but are a product of government. The problem with "laissez-faire" is not that it is unjust or harmful to poor people, but that it is a misdescription of any system of liberty, including free markets. Markets and wealth depend on government.

The misunderstanding is not innocuous. It blinds people to the omnipresence of government help for those who are doing well and makes it appear that those who are doing poorly, and complaining about it, are seeking a set of handouts. The New Deal vindicated these basic claims, and the Second Bill of Rights grew out of them. Doris Kearns Goodwin writes sensitively and acutely about Roosevelt. But she misses the point when she says of the Second Bill: "Nor had he ever been so explicit in linking together the negative liberty from government achieved in the old Bill of Rights to the positive liberty through government to be achieved in the new Bill of Rights."[49] This opposition between "liberty from government" and "liberty through government" misconceives what Roosevelt's presidency was all about.

LIBERALISM AND REALISM

The attack on the idea of laissez-faire has a long legacy in liberal thought. Jeremy Bentham, the father of utilitarianism, wrote, "Property and law are born together, and die together. Before the laws were made there was no property; take away the laws, and all property ceases."[50] This basic claim was an important strain of legal realism, the most influential movement in early twentieth-century America law. The realists, most notably law professors Robert Hale and Morris Cohen, insisted that markets and property depend on legal rules.[51] What people have is a reflection not of nature or custom but of governmental choices. This is so always, and simply as a matter of fact. Ownership rights are legal creations. In the New Deal, the realists were vindicated. Many of the legal realists found prominent positions in the Roosevelt administration.

For the realists, the most serious problem with the idea of laissez-faire was that the basic idea was simply a myth, a tangle of confusions. As Hale wrote, "The dependence of present economic conditions, in part at least, on the government's past policy concerning the distribution of the public domain, must be obvious. *Laissez-faire* is a utopian dream which never has been and never can be realized."[52] Supreme Court Justice Oliver Wendell Holmes Jr., in some ways the first legal realist, wrote in one of his most profound aphorisms (a near haiku): "Property, a creation of law, does not arise from value, although exchangeable—a matter of fact."[53] Holmes proclaimed that property and value are a product of legal rules, not of purely private interactions, still less of nature. Economic value does not predate law; it is created by law. And all this, wrote Holmes, was simply "a matter of fact."

The realists urged that government and law are omnipresent—that if some people have a lot and others a little, law is a large part of the reason. They complained that we ignore the extent to which we have what we have, and do what we do, only because of the law. They contended that people tend to see as "voluntary" and "free" interactions that are shot through with coercion. In their view, the law of property, contract, and tort are social creations that allocate certain rights to some people and deny them to others. These forms of law represent government "intervention" into the economy. They are coercive to the extent that they prohibit people from engaging in desired activities. If homeless people lack a place to live, it is not because of God's will or nature. It is because the rules of property will be invoked and enforced to evict them, if necessary by force. If employees have to work long hours and receive little money, it is in large part because of the prevailing rules of property and contract. The realists believed that private property is fine, even good, but they denied that the rules of property could be identified with liberty. Sometimes, those rules disserved liberty.

Robert Hale set forth these ideas with particular clarity. Hale wrote against the background of the political struggle over government efforts to set minimum wages and regulate prices, a struggle he believed was being waged on false premises. His special target was the view that governmental restrictions on market prices should be seen as illegitimate regulatory interference in the private sphere. This, said Hale, was an exceedingly confused way to describe the problem. Regulatory interference was already there:

> The right of ownership in a manufacturing plant is . . . a privilege to operate the plant, plus a privilege not to operate it, plus a right to keep others from operating, plus a power to acquire all the rights of ownership in the products. . . . This power is a power to release a pressure which the law of property exerts on the liberty of others. If the pressure is great, the owner may be able to compel the others to pay him a big price for their release; if the pressure is slight, he can collect but a small income from his ownership. *In either case, he is paid for releasing a pressure exerted by the government—the law. The law has delegated to him a discretionary power over the rights and duties of others.*[54]

Warren Samuels nicely summarized Hale's view: "Laissez faire does not mean no government, but really governmental indifference to the effects of artificial . . . coercive restraints partly grounded on government itself."[55] As Hale put it, "The distribution of wealth at any given time is not exclusively the result of individual efforts under a system of government neutrality."[56] And constraints on the freedom of nonowners were an omnipresent result of property law: "To insist that 'a free American has the right to labor without any other's leave' . . . is to insist on a doctrine which involves the dangerously radical consequence of the abolition of private ownership of productive equipment, or else the equally dangerous doctrine that everyone should be guaranteed the ownership of some such equipment."[57] In free markets, people do not really have the right to work "without any other's leave." Because of property rights, people can work only with the "leave" of others.

In a remarkable step, then, Hale argued that property rights were in effect a delegation of public power—a delegation to private people by government. In so arguing, Hale did not argue against property rights. Instead he sought to draw attention to the fact that property owners are, in effect, given a set of powers by law. If you have property, then you have *sovereignty*, a kind of official power vindicated by government, over that property. In these circumstances, Hale found it almost comical that some people complained about restrictions on property rights. In his view, a limitation on the delegation of power—in the form, for example, of a curtailment of "the incomes of property owners"—is "in substance curtailing the salaries of public officials or pensioners."[58]

Or consider these startlingly unambiguous words, from an unsigned student essay written in 1935: "Justification for this purported refusal to supervise the ethics of the market place is sought in doctrines of *laissez-faire. . . . In general, the freedom from regulation postulated by laissez faire adherents is demonstrably nonexistent and virtually inconceivable. Bargaining power exists only because of government protection of the property rights bargained,* and is properly subject to government control."[59] The same point lies behind this suggestion: "Those who denounce state intervention are the ones who most frequently and successfully invoke it. The cry of laissez faire mainly goes up from the ones who, if really 'let alone,' would instantly lose their wealth-absorbing power."[60]

In making these claims, the legal realists did not deny the possibility that some rights are, in a sense, "natural" or even God-given. Many liberals believe exactly that. Nothing in the realists' arguments should be seen as taking a stand on that question. They were not urging that as a matter of principle, rights come from government. They were urging instead that in actual life, people are able to have rights, and to enjoy them, only because law and government are present. We can speak all we like of natural or God-given rights, but without public protection of private property, people's holdings are inevitably at great risk. Whatever the source of rights in principle, legal protection is indispensable to make rights real in the world. Those who complain of "government," and who argue that they want merely to fend for themselves, ignore this point at their (literal) peril.

The realists' claims on this count were extremely prominent in America between 1910 and 1940. Hayek himself reminded his readers that the functioning of competition "depends, above all, on the existence of an appropriate legal system, a legal system designed both to preserve competition and to make it operate as beneficially as possible."[61] He urged that it "is by no means sufficient that the law should recognize the principle of private property and freedom of contract; much depends on the precise definition of the right of property as applied to different things."[62] Recall Hayek's emphatic statement that "in no system that could be rationally defended would the state just do nothing. An effective competitive system needs an intelligently designed and continuously adjusted legal framework as much as any other."[63] The real battle was not between those who favor "government intervention" and those who reject it. The question was how the legal framework should be "intelligently designed and continuously adjusted." Opposition to government intervention is a smoke screen, concealing that question.

ROOSEVELT'S LIBERALISM

The attack on laissez-faire ultimately made its way into the White House. Roosevelt made the point indirectly in his critique in 1934 of the idea of "the self-supporting man." He stressed that "without the help of thousands of others, any one of us would die, naked and starved. Consider the bread upon our table, the clothes upon our backs, the luxuries that make life pleasant; how many men worked in sunlit fields, in dark mines, in the fierce heat of molten metal, and among the looms and wheels of count-less factories, in order to create them for our use and enjoyment."[64] Still, this reminder of human interdependence did not refer to law and govern-ment. That point was made explicit in his early complaint, in accepting the Democratic nomination, that some leaders refer to "economic laws—sacred, inviolable, unchangeable," and his pragmatic response, that "while they prate of economic laws, men and women are starving."[65] Hence his plea that we "must lay hold of the fact that economic laws are not made by nature. They are made by human beings."[66] When people starve, it is a result of social choices, not anything sacred or inevitable.

Or consider Roosevelt's Commonwealth Club address in 1932, where he emphasized the view, which he attributed to Thomas Jefferson, "that the exercise of . . . property rights might so interfere with the rights of the indi-vidual that the government, without whose assistance the property rights could not exist, must intervene, not to destroy individualism but to protect it."[67] The key point here is that without government's assistance, property rights could not exist. When those governmentally conferred rights in fact "interfere with the rights of the individual," then governmental interven-tion is necessary to protect individualism itself. The legal realists could not have said it better.

Consider as well Roosevelt's emphasis on "this man-made world of ours" in advocating social security legislation.[68] He is arguing that poverty is a by-product of a human-created system, not a natural fact: "I decline to accept present conditions as inevitable or beyond control."[69] The same position was codified in the preamble to the most important piece of New Deal labor legislation, the Norris-LaGuardia Act: "Whereas under prevailing economic conditions, *developed with the aid of governmental authority for owners of prop-erty to organize in the corporate and other forms of ownership association*, the

individual worker is commonly helpless to exercise actual liberty of contract and to protect his freedom of labor, and thereby to obtain acceptable
terms and conditions of employment."[70]

To the extent, then, that property rights played a role in market arrangements—as they inevitably did—those arrangements were creatures of law,
including most notably property law, which gave some people a right to
exclude others from "their" land and resources.[71] Market wages and hours
were a result of legal rules conferring rights of ownership. Considered in this
light, minimum wage legislation did not superimpose regulation on a realm
of purely voluntary interactions, but merely substituted one form of regulation for another. It is in this sense that the notion of "laissez-faire" stands
revealed as myth. A system of free markets rests on a set of legal rules establishing who can do what, and enforcing those principles through the courts.

The New Deal liberals thought this was a simple descriptive point—as
Holmes put it, "a matter of fact." To say that government intervention is
pervasive and that no one is against it is not to say that any particular
form of intervention is good or bad. The real question is the pragmatic
one: What form of intervention best promotes human interests? When one
regulatory system is superimposed on another, it does not follow that all
bets are off or that we cannot evaluate these systems in constitutional terms
or for their effectiveness in diminishing or increasing human liberty. A system of private property is good for individuals and for societies, and the fact
that it is created by law does not suggest otherwise.

But in the face of the Great Depression, it seemed a kind of cruel joke
to maintain that free markets were sufficient to ensure either liberty or
prosperity. As Roosevelt saw it, people in desperate conditions lack freedom. New initiatives, responding to the problem of pervasive deprivation,
seemed indispensable. The question was whether they would work, and
this could not be answered by dogmas and abstractions. As Hale wrote,
"The next step is to . . . realize that the question of maintenance or the
alteration of our institutions must be discussed on its pragmatic merits,
not dismissed on the ground that they are the inevitable outcome of free
society."[72] The legal realist Morris Cohen, writing just before the New Deal,
put the point similarly: "The recognition of private property as a form of
sovereignty is not itself an argument against it. . . . It is necessary to apply to
the law of property all those considerations of social ethics and enlightened

public policy which ought to be brought to the discussion of any just form of government."[73]

To Roosevelt, that evaluation would be unabashedly empirical and experimental. It would avoid theories and dogmas, and it would look to see what sorts of programs actually helped people in the world. Its character is reflected in Roosevelt's apparently offhand but extremely revealing comment during a press conference: "Obviously a farm bill is in the nature of an experiment. We all recognize that. . . . If the darn thing doesn't work, we can say so quite frankly, but at least try it."[74] With this pragmatic reassessment, it is possible to understand the New Dealers' belief that certain measures that reduced the wealth of rich people were not an intrusion on rights—and that other measures, increasing the opportunities and wealth of poor people, were necessary to protect rights. Wealth did not come from nature or from the sky. It was made possible by legal arrangements. And if new legal arrangements diminished that wealth for some, they were not objectionable for that reason. In Roosevelt's words, "The thing that matters in any industrial system is what it does actually to human beings."[75]

NEW DEAL LIBERALISM AND DELIBERATIVE DEMOCRACY

In an important sense, the New Deal deepened the liberal commitment to deliberative democracy. For the original framers of the U.S. Constitution, it was exceedingly important to produce a political order that combined reflectiveness and reason-giving with a degree of popular responsiveness. Public officials were to be accountable, to be sure, and also to be removable by elections; the framers were committed to democracy in that sense. But majorities were feared as well; they were not permitted to rule simply because they were majorities. On the contrary, the constitutional system created a kind of republic of reasons—a system of checks and balances that would increase the likelihood of reflective judgments. Alexander Hamilton spoke most clearly on the point, urging that the "differences of opinion, and the jarring of parties in [the legislative] department of the government . . . often promote deliberation and circumspection; and serve to check the excesses of the majority."[76]

A similar point emerges from one of the most illuminating early debates, raising the question whether the bill of rights should include a "right to instruct" representatives. That right was defended with the claim that citizens of a particular region ought to have the authority to bind their representatives about how to vote. This argument might appear reasonable as a way of improving the political accountability of representatives. So it seemed to many at the time. Indeed, I suspect that many people, in America and elsewhere, would favor the "right to instruct" today. Shouldn't representatives do as their constituents wish? But there is a problem with this view, especially in an era in which political interest was closely aligned with geography. It is likely that the citizens of a particular region, influenced by one another's views, might end up with indefensible positions, very possibly as a result of its own insularity. In rejecting the right to instruct, Roger Sherman emphasized the importance of political deliberation: "The words are calculated to mislead the people, by conveying an idea that they have a right to control the debates of the Legislature. This cannot be admitted to be just, because it would destroy the object of their meeting. I think, when the people have chosen a representative, it is his duty to meet others from the different parts of the Union, and consult, and agree with them on such acts as are for the general benefit of the whole community. If they were to be guided by instructions, there would be no use in deliberation."[77]

Sherman's words reflect the founders' general receptivity to deliberation among people who are quite diverse and who disagree on issues both large and small. Indeed, it was through deliberation among such persons that "such acts as are for the general benefit of the whole community" would emerge. It is instructive in this light to understand the framers' preference for a republican system, involving deliberation among elected officials, over a more populist system, in which citizen desires would be less "filtered" through representatives. We can better appreciate the framers' enthusiasm for republican institutions if we see that they hoped that their design would simultaneously protect against unjustified passions and ensure a large measure of diversity in government. In this way, they hoped to structure public discussion such that it would ensure better decisions.

The Constitution was, of course, written against the legacy of English monarchy. A not-much-noticed provision reveals a great deal about the document's general goals and about liberalism in general: it forbids the government to grant "titles of nobility." In the framers' generation, preexisting notions of natural hierarchy came under siege, with a novel and revolutionary insistence that culture was, as the historian Gordon Wood put it, "truly man-made."[78] For the American revolutionaries, the problem with the monarchical legacy consisted of its acceptance, as natural, of practices and injustices that could not be rationally justified. America's liberal republicanism, in the Revolution and the founding period, consisted in part of a focus on this problem.

The New Dealers greatly deepened the liberal commitment to deliberative democracy. They did this by insisting that the existing distributions of wealth and opportunities were also man-made, and that economic facts were not dictated by nature. They insisted that respect for existing practices must depend on the reasons that could be brought forward on their behalf. The process of deliberation through democratic organs would therefore include an assessment of whether the legal rules already in place served liberty, welfare, or democracy itself. In this way, the New Deal period carried forward and made new one of the oldest themes in American history. Enormous changes followed from these understandings.

WHITHER?

Franklin Delano Roosevelt wrote, or participated in the writing of, countless articles, essays, and speeches. But before he became president, he produced only one book. In 1926, at the age of forty-four, Roosevelt lectured at the Alumni War Memorial Foundation at Milton Academy in Massachusetts. The slim volume that resulted from those lectures is called *Whither Bound?*.[79]

Much of the book is devoted to an account of the likely future and to the need for an optimistic attitude toward it. Roosevelt speaks disapprovingly of an imaginary "citizen of this land" who is "sorely troubled . . . of gloomy religion, of copybook sentiment, of life by precept," who "lived as had his fathers before him."[80] This imaginary citizen is hostile to social and scientific change; he is alarmed by technology and even more by challenges to the existing social structure. "Women—think of it, Women!—were commencing to take positions in offices and industrial plants, and demanding—a very few of them—things called political rights."[81] For Roosevelt, the coming changes should be seen as opportunities, full of promise. "Some among us would stop the clock, call a halt to all this change, and then in some well-thought-out way bring back an orderly, defined way of life . . . —the 'good old days' restored."[82]

Roosevelt, a liberal in spirit, ridicules this route. He foresees that medicine will conquer many old forms of disease, with the result that "we begin to expect to live to a ripe old age by right, and not by mere chance."[83] (He was right.) He foresees changes in transportation that will make current capacities appear "childish within our own lives."[84] (He was right.) More remarkably, he foresees a time "when any two persons on earth will be able to be completely present to one another" in less than a second.[85] (Right again.) "I wonder, indeed, if the thought of this probability is one whit more startling to us to-night than the thought of the human voice carried over the telephone was to our grandfathers?"[86]

All the trends, Roosevelt suggests, are "toward the greater unification of mankind."[87] Human diseases are increasingly spreading from one nation to another. "Power is exported. Capital is international."[88] As a result, isolation "of individual nations will be as difficult in this future as would be the isolation of New England or the South to-day."[89] This is true in economics, science, and even law, where experiments in one national unit "are influenced by experiments in other units."[90]

In his last few pages, Roosevelt turns from prognostication to political and moral issues. Here he offers a plea. The idea of "service of mankind," he urges, while much discussed, is "still in its infancy of development. True service will not come until all the world recognizes all the rest of the world as one big family."[91] It is not enough to help a fellow human being out of a sense of duty. Assistance should be provided not from duty but "as an interest. How many of us lend helping hands to people we do not like, people who do not 'belong to our crowd,' people whom we subconsciously hope we may never see again?"[92] Increasingly, Roosevelt contends, "we become interdependent. Communities merge into states, states into nations, nations into families of peoples."[93] The real task is to "take our part positively and not negatively."[94]

In the decade that followed, America's public institutions were radically transformed under Roosevelt's leadership. Under New Deal liberalism, the federal government assumed powers formerly believed to rest with the states. The presidency grew dramatically in stature and importance; it became the principal seat of American democracy. A newly developed bureaucracy, including independent regulatory commissions, was put in place. The foundations of the transformation are best captured in a changing understanding of rights, often in the form of helping hands. In Roosevelt's view, desperate conditions are not inescapable by-products of our economic order; they are entirely preventable by an alert government.

"The laws of economics are not made by nature; they are made by human beings."[95] Roosevelt insisted on opportunities for all and on a cushion for those at the bottom of this "man-made world of ours."[96] He organized his claims under the rubric of security, which he saw as indispensable to freedom.

Roosevelt believed that by 1944, the United States had "come to accept" the Second Bill of Rights. Badly scarred by the Great Depression and a world war, the nation was now committed to freedom from want and freedom from fear, which it saw as intertwined. The Second Bill was necessary to achieve both forms of freedom. Following James Madison's hopes for the original Bill of Rights, Roosevelt hoped that the Second Bill would play a large role in politics and even culture. Americans had come to understand that whatever their rhetoric, no one is against government intervention, and that the idea of laissez-faire is a hopeless misdescription of their system. Those with wealth and property are advantaged, every day of every year, by government and by law. The people who complain most vociferously about intervention by government are usually its principal beneficiaries. Far from being self-sufficient, they owe their own well-being at least in part to government assistance. By 1944, Roosevelt urged, the real task was one of implementing the Second Bill.

This task remains incomplete. To be sure, the Second Bill helps to account for central features of modern American government. The Affordable Care Act can be seen as a recognition of "the right to adequate medical care and the opportunity to achieve and enjoy good health." The right to education is firmly entrenched at the state level; it receives explicit recognition in many state constitutions. The Supreme Court has said that the federal Constitution itself gives some protection to this right, and in any case the national government is committed, in broad principle, to ensuring a decent education for all. In the same vein, the right to be free from monopoly is a firmly established part of contemporary government. The laws forbidding conspiracy in restraint of trade are nearly as secure as the right to free speech itself. So too, the Social Security Act has the essential characteristics of a commitment. In public life, no serious person can argue for its abolition. Of course, politicians differ about how, exactly, to keep that commitment. But when officials are seen to question the commitment itself, the public reacts as if a fundamental principle were at stake. In any case, large-scale national programs do a great deal to provide food, housing, employment, and even health care. In all of these ways, we live under Roosevelt's Constitution whether we know it or not. The American Constitution has become, in crucial respects, his own.

But the triumph of Roosevelt's conception of liberalism is only partial. Too many of the nation's citizens neglect the extent to which their own well-being is a product of a system of government that benefits them every day. Too many Americans complain about "government intervention" without understanding that their own wealth and opportunities exist only because of that intervention. In a society that purports to prize opportunity for all, too many citizens lack a minimally fair chance. In the last decades, we have neglected some of our deepest ideals, with roots not merely in the New Deal but also in the Civil War and the founding period itself. The Second Bill of Rights is largely unknown.

The United States celebrates what it calls the Greatest Generation, the victors in World War II. Because of its achievements, its sacrifices, and its valor, the World War II generation deserves celebration. But it does not deserve sentimentality, romanticism, or ancestor worship. These could not be farther from its pragmatic and forward-looking spirit. In the midst of World War II, the greatest leader of that generation believed it had a project, one that was radically incomplete. That project, liberal in character, is best captured in the Second Bill of Rights.

There is an inextricable link between freedom from fear and freedom from want. People who want are frightened. Liberty and citizenship are rooted in security. The Second Bill of Rights should be claimed in its nation of origin, and all over the globe.

8 OPPORTUNITY

My topic here is liberalism and opportunity, but let us start with Connie Converse, who is widely known, of course, as the most original, and perhaps the greatest, of the folk singers of the 1950s and 1960s. Described as "the first singer-songwriter," she is often ranked with Bob Dylan, whom she preceded. She greatly influenced not only Dylan, but also Joan Baez, Joni Mitchell, Judy Collins, the Beatles, the Rolling Stones, James Taylor, Cat Stevens, and Crosby, Stills, Nash & Young—and more recently, Aimee Mann, Beyoncé, Kanye West, and Taylor Swift.

You undoubtedly know one of her greatest hits, "Roving Woman," whose defiant sensibility defined an era, and which can be heard on the radio even today:

> People say a roving woman
> Is likely not to be better than she ought to be;
> So, when I stray away from where I've got to be,
> Someone always takes me home.

> A lady never should habituate saloons,
> And that is where I find myself on many afternoons.
> But just as I begin to blow away the foam,
> Someone tips his hat to me and takes me home. . . .

> Don't see why they always do it—
> Can't be vanity; must be sheer humanity—
> When some kind soul remarks with great urbanity:
> "Lady, let me take you home."

> Of course, there's bound to be some little aftermath
> That makes a pleasant ending for the straight and narrow path.

And as I go to sleep, I cannot help but think
How glad I am that I was saved from cards and drink

In the 1950s, people were both scandalized and delighted by the sexy mischief here: "Of course, there's bound to be some little aftermath / That makes a pleasant ending for the straight and narrow path / And as I go to sleep, I cannot help but think / How glad I am that I was saved from cards and drink." And, of course, the song's meaning is much debated. Is it a feminist anthem, or just the opposite? What exactly is Converse saying about men? Is she fond of them? Is she contemptuous? ("Can't be vanity; / must be sheer humanity— / When some kind soul remarks with great urbanity: / 'Lady, let me take you home.'")

In academic circles, Converse's song is generally believed to be an ironic, upbeat celebration of female agency—something that presaged certain forms of liberal feminism today. (Consider here Beyoncé's off-the-charts admiration for Converse.) It is agreed that "Roving Woman" is much subtler, and more interesting, than Helen Reddy's "I Am Woman," though Reddy claims to have been directly inspired by Converse and to have written her own anthem in direct, hard-hitting response to Converse's very different one.

You almost certainly know Converse's haunting, mournful "One by One," that aching tale of loneliness and alienation:

We go walking in the dark.
We go walking out at night.

And it's not as lovers go,
Two by two, to and fro;
But it's one by one—

One by one in the dark.

"One by One" has mystery at its core. Is it about lost love? Or a love that was desperately hoped for, but that never was? Is it a plea? An attempted seduction? A love letter? Whatever else it is, it is surely a deliberate play on the end of *Paradise Lost* and hence on the Fall: "They hand in hand with wandring steps and slow / Through Eden took thir solitarie way."

Converse is not only a pioneering folksinger. When she "went electric" in 1965, she and Dylan built the foundations of modern rock music. On this, she followed Dylan by a few months, though she preceded him in writing new folk songs. She is often taught in literature courses, and some people believe that in the fullness of time, a Nobel Prize is not out of the question.

"DOZENS OF FANS ALL OVER THE WORLD"

Okay, okay, I have been lying; I described a counterfactual world. But I didn't only lie, and the world I described is not entirely counterfactual. Connie Converse was indeed a folk singer in the 1950s. "Roving Woman" and "One by One" are real songs, and Converse wrote them, but she never released a commercial album. She never played to a large audience. She had no hits. She played mostly to friends and family. (In fact, it would be excessive to say that she played to "audiences.") Converse tried hard to make it, and she did attract some interest from well-connected people, some of whom tried to help her. But she was never "discovered."

As she put it, "I have dozens of fans all over the world." That is the same sensibility that produced the mischievous, double-take-producing line, "People say a roving woman / Is likely not to be better than she ought to be."

Startlingly, Converse appeared on national television—but just once, with Walter Cronkite. There is no video or audio recording of her appearance (only photographs), and the appearance did not give her career any kind of boost. She was writing folk songs before people wrote folk songs. She didn't fit in any kind of niche. Was she a genius? Was she a victim of discrimination? What kind of discrimination? Was she before her time?

Frustrated by a decade of failure, she essentially stopped writing music in the late 1950s. In 1961, she moved from New York to Ann Arbor, Michigan, where she became managing editor of an academic journal. She left New York in the very same month that Bob Dylan arrived there. Apparently he never heard of her. (He did a bit better than she did.) She disappeared in 1974, at the age of fifty, when she left her home in Ann Arbor, in her Volkswagen Beetle. She wrote a number of opaque goodbye notes to friends and family, saying that she was returning to New York.

No one knows where she went or what happened to her. It is generally believed that she committed suicide. Neither her body nor her car was ever found. It is all a mystery.

MARGINALIZED TALENTS

But that is not the end of the story. Not close. On January 9, 2004, Gene Deitch, a famous cartoonist who was also an amateur recording engineer, was asked to appear on a radio show in New York—WYNC's *Spinning on Air*, hosted by David Garland. At eighty years old, Deitch had a lot of recordings. He sent a sample of what he had to Garland, who did not much like what he heard. But there was a single exception: Garland loved Connie Converse.

It turned out that when living in New York in the 1950s, Deitch had used a new tape recorder to capture the music of his guests at various small, informal gatherings he would organize. At one such gathering in 1954, Deitch recorded Converse. He told Garland that he had been stunned by what he heard, but that he failed to stay in touch with her, and that she had disappeared in the 1970s. Intrigued by the tale, Garland asked Deitch to talk on air about the mysterious Converse, and also to play some of her music. Deitch chose "One by One." He claimed that in 1954, those at his small gathering had fallen "in love with her music" and that Converse was a "lost genius." He spoke about her for about a minute.

That might have been the end of the matter. In a logical world, it probably ought to have been. But as it happened, Dan Dzula, a twenty-year-old college student in New York, was listening to that very episode of *Spinning on Air* while driving to his parents' house on a Sunday night. He was knocked out by what he heard. He absorbed "One by One" in stunned silence. As soon as he got home, Dzula tried to find out everything he could about Converse. What he found online was: nothing at all. Puzzled and rapt, he replayed the episode of *Spinning on Air* and eventually recorded, just for himself, Converse's rendition of "One by One."

After graduating from college, Dzula began work at a studio as an engineer, mixing and producing. He asked his college classmate, David Herman, to join him there. All the while, he continued to be intrigued by Converse and would occasionally play "One by One" for his friends. Again, in a logical world, that might also have been the end of matter. But on one afternoon, Dzula played the song for Herman, who immediately saw an opportunity: Shouldn't the two of them try to find Converse's songs? Shouldn't they compile and release a debut album, more than a half century after her death?

In 2007, Dzula wrote Deitch, volunteering to try to do exactly that. Deitch immediately sent a package to Dzula the next day, with seventeen songs by Converse. Dzula also engaged Converse's family, and her brother, the distinguished political scientist Philip Converse, was able to provide him with a number of recordings. In late 2008, Dzula and Herman decided to release Converse's music commercially. They began with a digital EP, consisting of only three songs. They posted a link to it on social media, alongside a short account of Converse's life. The reaction was spectacular. Encouraged, they produced a full-length album, How Sad, How Lovely. In 2009, Garland devoted an entire episode to Converse. The album has turned out to be a huge success. The album has been streamed on Spotify more than sixteen million times.

Converse isn't quite in the canon of folk music, but she is getting there. If she does, it might be because of Howard Fishman's riveting book on Converse, *To Anyone Who Ever Asks*, which was published in 2023.[1] Fishman happened to hear a song of hers—"Talkin' Like You," from *How Sad, How Lovely*—at a party in 2010, and he has been obsessed with her ever since. His book is a celebration, a detective story, a lament, and an effort to correct what he sees as a shocking injustice. In Fishman's account, Converse really was a genius, and she should have been recognized as such in her time. Fishman quotes Ellen Stekert, a scholar of folk music: "She was the female Bob Dylan. She was even better than him, as a lyricist and composer, but she didn't have his showbiz savvy, and she wasn't interested in writing protest songs."[2] Fishman says something similar, pointing to the role of serendipity: "Dylan was in the right place at the right time. Converse was not."[3]

Stekert's statement is too strong. Converse was not the female Bob Dylan, and she was certainly not better than he was. Still, she was original, and she was poetic. She visited the depths. She was heartbreaking, and she was funny. She was much more interesting, and much more surprising, than Joan Baez or Judy Collins. Both of them were and are amazing, but Converse was better. It is easy to imagine a counterfactual world in which she really did define her era. In that sense, Fishman has it just right.

Why had no one heard of her until 2008? Fishman quotes her brother as saying, "Sis did not miss the Big Time by a whole lot." Fishman himself thinks that Converse "was anything *but* lucky."[4] Her appearance with Walter Cronkite "was almost the lucky break she needed. Almost."[5] He argues that Converse had a deficit of one thing above all: connections. Here's how he ends his book: "My hope is that I have somehow at least served as a worthy shepherd, and that others will follow along, joining in the parade behind Converse as she makes her way at last to the place she belongs, to the table of great American artists and thinkers."[6]

Fishman also has something to ask: "How many Connie Converses are there out there—marginalized talents waiting to be heard; artists and thinkers lacking the emotional tools, the encouragement, the self-esteem, the community, needed to thrive?"[7] That is a profoundly liberal question. We will get to that, and return to Mill and Rawls, shortly.

THE MUSIC LAB

A number of years ago, three social scientists—Matthew Salganik, Duncan Watts, and Peter Dodds—investigated the sources of cultural success and failure.[8] Their starting point was that those who sell books, movies, television shows, and songs often have a great deal of trouble predicting what will succeed. Even experts make serious mistakes. Some products are far more successful than anticipated, whereas others are far less so. This seems to suggest, very simply, that those that succeed must be far better than those that do not. But if they are so much better, why are predictions so difficult? We know that a new book by Stephen King is likely to do well; we know that a new song by Taylor Swift is likely to be a hit. We know that a horrible book or a horrible song is probably doomed. But there doesn't appear to be a lot more that we know. Who knew that a 2009 album by Connie Converse, a singer who disappeared decades before, would go viral on Spotify? For that matter, who could be sure that in the 1950s, Converse would never make it?

To explore the sources of cultural success and failure, Salganik and his coauthors created an artificial music market on a preexisting website. The site offered people an opportunity to hear forty-eight real but unknown songs by real but unknown bands. One song, by a band called Calefaction, was "Trapped in an Orange Peel." Another, by Hydraulic Sandwich, was "Separation Anxiety." Another song, by Silverfox, was "Gnaw." Another, by Fading Through, was "Wish Me Luck." Another, by Salute the Dawn, was "I Am Error."

The experimenters randomly sorted half of about fourteen thousand site visitors into an "independent judgment" group, in which they were invited to listen to brief excerpts, to rate songs, and to decide whether to download them. From those seven thousand visitors, Salganik and his coauthors could obtain a clear sense of what people liked best. The other seven thousand visitors were sorted into a "social influence" group, which was exactly the same except in just one respect: the social influence group could see how many times each song had been downloaded by other participants.

Those in the social influence group were also randomly assigned to one of eight subgroups, *in which they could see only the number of downloads in their own subgroup*. In those different subgroups, it was inevitable that different songs would attract different initial numbers of downloads as a result of serendipitous or random factors. For example, "Trapped in an Orange Peel" might attract strong support from the first listeners in one subgroup, whereas it might attract no such support in another. "Wish Me Luck" might be unpopular in its first hours in one subgroup but attract a great deal of favorable attention in another.

The research questions were simple. Would the initial numbers affect where songs would end up in terms of total number of downloads? Would the initial numbers affect the ultimate rankings of the forty-eight songs? Would the eight subgroups differ in those rankings?

You might hypothesize that after a period, quality would always prevail—that in this relatively simple setting, where various extraneous factors (such as reviews, energetic managers, radio placements, concerts, and word of mouth) were not at work, the popularity of the songs, as measured by their download rankings, would be roughly the same in the independent group and in all eight of the social influence groups. (Recall that for the purposes of the experiment, quality is being measured solely by reference to what happened within the control group.)

It's a tempting hypothesis, but that is not at all what happened. "Wish Me Luck" could be a major hit or a miserable flop, depending on whether a lot of other people initially downloaded it and were seen to have done so. To a significant degree, everything turned on initial popularity. Almost any song could end up popular or not, depending on whether or not the first visitors liked it.

Connie Converse was not, of course, in the music lab experiment, or in anything very close to it. She could not benefit from the internet, and her songs were not on some kind of publicly available list. But in some larger sense, she failed, during the 1950s and 1960s, because of the absence of early downloads. For reasons that remain mysterious, her appearance on national television attracted essentially no attention. (Was she nervous? Did she perform poorly?) Until decades after her disappearance, she found no sponsors who were able to start some kind of bandwagon effect on her behalf. It might be tempting to say that she was "before her time," and to suggest that if she had started five years later, she would have become a star. But that is speculative in the extreme. Who knows? It is equally plausible to say that in the end, she was not unlike those songs in the music lab experiment that ended up tanking simply because they did not get early support.

If that seems doubtful, compare a tale told in 2012, when the Oscar for Best Documentary was awarded to *Searching for Sugar Man*.[9] The film focuses on an unsuccessful Detroit singer-songwriter named Sixto Rodriguez, also known as Sugar Man, who released two albums in the early 1970s. Almost no one bought his albums, and his label dropped him. In crucial respects, Rodriguez was a lot like Converse. Having failed, Rodriguez stopped making records and sought work as a demolition man. His two albums were forgotten. A family man with three daughters, Rodriguez was hardly miserable. But working in demolition, he struggled.

The film suggests that having abandoned his musical career, Rodriguez had no idea that he had become a spectacular success in South Africa—a giant, a legend, comparable to the Beatles, Bob Dylan, and the Rolling Stones. People said his name slowly and with awe, even reverence: "Rodriguez." Describing him as "the soundtrack to our lives," South Africans bought hundreds of thousands of copies of his albums, starting in the 1970s.[10] His South African fans speculated about his mysterious departure from the musical scene. Why did he suddenly stop making records? According to one rumor, he burned himself to death onstage. *Searching for Sugar Man* is about the contrast between the failed career of Detroit's obscure demolition man and the renown of South Africa's mysterious rock icon.

The film is easily taken as a real-world fairy tale and barely believable. It does not attempt to explain the contrast between Rodriguez's general failure and his extraordinary success in South Africa. We might be tempted to think that (for example) his music resonated with the South African culture. Perhaps so. It might seem plausible to speculate that in a period of racial division and cultural upheaval, there was something about Rodriguez that connected deeply with South Africa. But an alternative explanation is that *Searching for Sugar Man* depicts a real-life version of the music lab experiment. Perhaps Rodriguez found himself in numerous counterfactual worlds, and because of an absence of early downloads in most, he was forgotten in nearly all of them. But in one, early downloads were numerous, and he became an icon.

The tale of Sixto Rodriguez is closely analogous to that of Connie Converse. With Rodriguez, success and failure were across space: spectacular fame in South Africa (and also Australia, as it happens), and ignoble failure everywhere else. With Converse, success and failure were across time: adulation decades after her (probable?) death, and ignoble failure while she was writing songs. Intrinsic quality matters, of course. But it is not nearly enough.

LIBERALISM AND OPPORTUNITY

In the domain of innovation in general, social scientists refer to "lost Einsteins"—those "who would have had highly impactful inventions had they been exposed to innovation in childhood."[11] The emphasis here is on demographic characteristics, such as race, gender, and socioeconomic status, and on the contributions of role models and network effects to success. Countless potential innovators, in science, business, and elsewhere, were deprived in some way, or were born in a family that failed to nourish their talents, or did not find the right role models, or did not benefit from relevant networks. As a result, they never innovated. Or they might have innovated, but no one ever noticed. Or they might have innovated, but no one, or almost no one, noticed until long after their death. (Think Bach, van Gogh, Herman Melville, William Blake, Emily Dickinson, Kafka, Robert Johnson—and Connie Converse.)

One of the central goals of liberalism, and of the liberal tradition, is to undo the relevant forms of subjugation, which is why Mill's *The Subjection of Women* is a canonical liberal text (and essential reading, not least for antiliberals). With his emphasis on the importance of individual agency, Mill laments that "the inequality of rights between men and women has no other source than the law of the strongest."[12] In a key passage, Mill writes: "What is the peculiar character of the modern world—the difference that chiefly distinguishes modern institutions, modern social ideas, modern life itself, from those of times long past? It is that human beings are no longer born to their place in life, and chained down by an inexorable bond to the place they are born to, but are free to employ their faculties, and such favourable chances as offer, to achieve the lot which may appear to them most desirable."[13]

Mill's argument here is more subtle than the context might suggest. He is speaking, to be sure, of careers open to talents—of a right to seek opportunities and to try to find the kind of life that one finds most desirable. That is, he is pointing to the injustice of unwanted chains and bonds. But Mill is also careful to draw attention to the importance of "favourable chances." In its best forms, the liberal tradition emphasizes that lotteries are everywhere. It points to the place of favorable chances and the multiple forms they take. John Rawls's *A Theory of Justice* is the most sustained development of that point. It urges that principles of justice ought to be selected from what Rawls calls the *original position*, in which we know nothing about our own characteristics or our place in society—including our wealth, our opportunities, our tastes, our talents. Rawls argues that in the original position, our judgments are not distorted by characteristics that are irrelevant from the moral point of view, including what he calls the *natural lottery*, which refers to our genetic endowments (such as intelligence and musical ability). In giving a central position to the original position, Rawls helped define a prominent form of liberalism (and my favorite).

Connie Converse won the natural lottery (she was phenomenally gifted), but she lost a lot of other lotteries. Was she a victim of sex discrimination? Undoubtedly. Did she fail in the music business because she was female? Possibly. She certainly had long strings of bad luck.

The music lab is everywhere. It follows that when potential innovators end up lost, it is not only because of demographic characteristics, but also because of a host of innumerable other factors, which may not even be possible to identify, and which did not work in their favor. Aspiring innovators might not have found the right enemies, inspirations, or champions. They might not have been able to benefit from a network. Someone might not have given them a path, a smile at the right time, an infusion of energy, or a contract.

Jane Franklin, obscure sister of Benjamin Franklin, and perhaps as talented as he (who knows?), was much taken with the arguments of Richard Price, who was much focused on the importance of starting points, which doom so many.[14] "Dr. Price," Jane wrote to Benjamin, "thinks Thousands of Boyles Clarks and Newtons have Probably been lost to the world, and lived and died in Ignorance and meanness, merely for want of being Placed in favourable Situations, and Injoying Proper Advantages."[15] Jane's lament was personal. As Jill Lepore writes, Benjamin Franklin thought of his sister as his "Second Self," and of the family's seventeen (!) children, no two were more alike.[16] And while Benjamin became an icon, one of the leading

literary and scientific thinkers in the entire history of the American Republic, Jane's education was stunted, despite her keen interest in reading and
writing. Liberals hate that.

Jane Franklin's lament might seem to point to a tragedy, even to countless tragedies—not only for those who have been lost, but also to those
of us who have lost them. In many ways, that is indeed tragic. But it also
points to a possibility or perhaps an inspiration. Lost Einsteins might be
found again. In fact, they are being found every day. They are being found
in the same way that Connie Converse was found again. Liberals want to
reduce the likelihood that they will get lost in the first place.

EPILOGUE: FIRE AND HOPE

Some people believe that freedom is incompatible with order. They think that people will not choose well. They see freedom as a threat. When freedom of speech is shut down, that is a common reason. Many people believe that the rule of law is incompatible with security, and they suspend the rule of law in its name. Of course, many people deplore liberty because they seek to retain their power and their privilege.

Franklin Delano Roosevelt had something to say about this: "Yes, these men and their hypnotized followers call this a new order. It is not new and it is not order."[1] Recall Lincoln's words: "No man is good enough to govern another man, without that other's consent. I say this is the leading principle—the sheet anchor of American republicanism." The rights that liberals prize are an outgrowth of that principle: the right to vote, the right to free speech, the right to religious liberty, the right to due process of law. The right to private property is itself associated with Lincoln's sheet anchor. If you cannot own things, you are vulnerable to the power of others—above all, the government.

No ism can offer concrete solutions to concrete social and political problems. You can agree with Mill or Rawls without having clarity about how to approach climate change, artificial intelligence, or a proposed increase in the minimum wage. You can be a liberal without knowing what to think about immigration. You can believe in freedom of speech without knowing how to handle libel, commercial advertising, and pornography. You can believe in freedom of religion without knowing whether it is permissible to apply prohibitions on race and sex discrimination to religious schools.

In its early days, liberalism was full of fire. It is impossible to read Mill's *On Liberty* (1859) without feeling that fire: "If all mankind minus one, were of one opinion, and only one person were of the contrary opinion, mankind would be no more justified in silencing that one person, than he, if he had the power, would be justified in silencing mankind."[2] The same is true of *The Subjection of Women* (1869): "The legal subordination of one sex to the other . . . is wrong in itself and now one of the chief hindrances to human improvement."[3] Something similar can be said of Constant's *Principles of Politics Applicable to All Governments* (1815). Thus: "Political freedom would be a thing of no value if the rights of individuals were not sheltered from all violation. Any country where these rights are not respected is a country subjected to despotism, whatever the nominal organization of government may otherwise be. Till a few years ago these truths were universally recognized. Lasting errors and a long oppression, under wholly contrary pretexts and quite opposite banners, have thrown all ideas into confusion."[4]

Rawls's *A Theory of Justice* (1971) is much quieter, with its gentle final line: "Purity of heart, if one could attain it, would be to see clearly and to act with grace and self-command from this point of view."[5]

It would be extreme to say, with William Butler Yeats, that over a half-century after Rawls's great book, "The best lack all conviction, while the worst / Are full of passionate intensity." The best do not lack conviction. But it would not be extreme to say that some contemporary accounts of liberalism have a defensive quality; they seem a bit tired, passive, backward-looking, even nostalgic.

In law and politics, as in sports, the best offense is sometimes a good defense. Still, a defining feature of liberalism has always been its youth—its energy and fierceness, its delight in human agency, its openness to novelty and surprise, its high spirits, its opposition to cruelty, its capacity for indignation, its optimism, its continuing adventures in self-definition, its refusal to despair, its sense of mischief, its commitment to experiments in living.

Liberalism is full of hope. Hopeful people are remaking it every day.

ACKNOWLEDGMENTS

A few years ago, I started to write notes to myself about what liberalism was and wasn't. The little essay, if you can call it that, was titled *Why I Am a Liberal*. I was inspired by Friedrich Hayek's great essay, *Why I Am Not a Conservative*, which took the form of numbered paragraphs. What I wrote was in the nature of "notes to self"; I didn't know what, if anything, to do with them.

One day, I decided to send my document to two friends: Tyler Cowen and Bret Stephens. Tyler responded favorably and said I should publish that document. But where, I wondered? It seemed too academic for a magazine or a newspaper, and insufficiently academic for an academic journal. Bret thought that the document should become an essay and that the *New York Times* should publish it. I was not only honored but also amazed. What I sent him was (I thought) far too long to be published there, and also far too academic. But Bret's colleagues agreed with him, and the essay did indeed appear in the *Times* (on November 20, 2023). Special thanks to Vanessa Mobley for terrific editorial work.

The essay struck a nerve. Some people didn't much like it, and it endangered a friendship or two, but I received a large number of kind notes from people on the right and the left, saying that it captured much of what they thought—of what they were for and (especially) what they were against. Some people on the right wrote me to castigate the illiberal right. Some people on the left wrote me to castigate the illiberal left. There was a shared concern, I learned, about illiberalism and postliberalism. Chapter 1 is a greatly expanded version of the original essay, and it anchors the present volume.

I have many people to thank. For decades, Stephen Holmes has been teaching me about liberalism—for a number of blessed years when we were neighbors and friends in Chicago, and for a number of years from a distance. His work on the topic sets the standard. I hope I have not let my teacher down too badly. Catherine Woods, my editor, made the book better in innumerable ways. Sarah Chalfant, my agent, encouraged me to proceed, and saw, early on, what should be emphasized. Four reviewers offered detailed thoughts for improvements, and I am most grateful to them. Victoria Yu has been a partner on this project, as on several others, and I thank her for that partnership, and for extraordinary research assistance.

Since my early years as a law professor (the 1980s!), I have been exploring, in one way or another, issues that are central to liberalism—in part as it has long been understood, in part as it might be understood if liberalism were put in its most appealing form. I have drawn on some past writings here, while also substantially revising them and producing, I hope, a relatively unified text. Chapter 2 draws on *Experiments of Living Constitutionalism*, from 46 Harvard Journal of Law and Public Policy 1177 (2023). Chapter 3 draws on *John & Harriet: Still Mysterious*, from the New York Review of Books (2015). Chapter 4 draws on *The Rule of Law*, Harvard Journal of Law and Equality (2024). Chapter 5 draws on *Falsehoods and the First Amendment*, 33 Harvard Journal of Law and Technology 388 (2020). Chapter 6 draws on *Hayekian Behavioral Economics*, 7 Behavioral Public Policy 170 (2023). Chapter 7 grows out of a chapter in my book *The Second Bill of Rights* (2004). Chapter 8 draws on a discussion in my book *How to Become Famous* (2024). I am grateful to all for permissions to draw on that previous work here.

NOTES

PREFACE

1. George Orwell, *1984: A Novel* 220 (Signet Classics 1961) (1949).

2. Id. at 111.

3. Id. at 245.

4. A superb treatment of the theoretical issues is found in *Routledge Handbook of Illiberalism* (András Sajó, Renáta Uitz, and Stephen Holmes eds., 2022). Also superb, and pulling no punches, is Stephen Holmes, *The Anatomy of Antiliberalism* (1993). I am aware that antiliberals and postliberals do not like the punches, and I hope to have a few not-so-punchy things to say to them. Superb once more is Alan Ryan, *The Making of Modern Liberalism* (2012).

5. See the brilliant treatment in Helena Rosenblatt, *The Lost History of Liberalism: From Ancient Rome to the Twenty-First Century* (2018), from which I borrow heavily here.

6. See id. at 4, 52 (arguing that historically, "liberals ceaselessly advocated generosity, moral probity, and civic values" instead of "the atomistic individualism we hear of today").

7. See id. at 6 (explaining that there was a time when the "corresponding noun was 'liberality' and the word 'liberalism' did not yet exist").

8. See id. at 11–16 (describing how the "ancient view of liberality was not entirely lost [during the Middle Ages] but Christianized").

9. Id. at 17.

10. Id. at 18–19.

11. Id. at 22.

12. See id. at 8 ("The word 'liberalism' did not even exist until the early nineteenth century").

13. Id. at 29.

14. See id. (observing that "liberal-minded gentlemen advocated increasingly expansive notions of religious toleration," which they considered the "most 'just and liberal' policy for governments to adopt").

15. Id.

16. See id. at 36–40 (reporting that "Americans often boasted that their own constitutions were the most liberal in the world").

17. See id. at 42 ("The word itself was coined only around 1811" and owed "its birth to the French Revolution").

18. See generally id. at 49–55.

19. Id. at 53.

20. See id. at 65–67 (summarizing Constant's arguments in *Principles*).

21. See id. at 78–79 (surveying the *Historical Depiction*). On Constant, see Stephen Holmes, *Benjamin Constant and the Making of Modern Liberalism* (1984).

22. See generally John Rawls, *A Theory of Justice* (1971).

23. Id. at 60.

24. Id. at 61.

25. John Rawls, *Political Liberalism* 137 (1996).

26. Id. at xviii–xix.

CHAPTER 1

1. James D. Fearon, *Deliberation as Discussion*, in *Deliberative Democracy* 44, 53–55 (Jon Elster ed., 1983).

2. John Stuart Mill, *On Liberty* 67 (2nd ed. 1859).

3. Abraham Lincoln, Speech on the Kansas-Nebraska Act at Peoria, Illinois, in *Abraham Lincoln: Speeches and Writings 1832–1858* 307, 328 (1989) (emphasis in original).

4. Abraham Lincoln, Letter to Albert G. Hodges (Apr. 4, 1854) (available at the American Presidency Project), https://www.presidency.ucsb.edu/documents/letter -albert-g-hodges.

5. See John Stuart Mill, *The Subjection of Women* (1869).

6. Id. at 1. Philip Pettit has argued powerfully and in many places for a conception of freedom as nondomination. For a crisp treatment, see Philip Pettit, *The Instability of Freedom as Noninterference: The Case of Isaiah Berlin*, 121 Ethics 693 (2011); Philip Pettit, *On the People's Terms: A Republican Theory and Model of Democracy* (2013).

Pettit's work has much influenced this book, though I leave him mostly in the background.

7. See Cass R. Sunstein, *The Anticaste Principle*, 92 Mich. L. Rev. 2410, 2410–2455 (1994); for a valuable angle on this, see Pettit, *The Instability of Freedom*, supra note 6. Those who lack capacity present special cases; consider young children.

8. United States v. Schwimmer, 279 U.S. 644, 654–55 (1929) (Holmes, J., dissenting).

9. Helena Rosenblatt, *The History of Illiberalism*, in *Routledge Handbook of Illiberalism* (András Sajó, Renáta Uitz, and Stephen Holmes eds., 2022), at 22.

10. Id.

11. West Virginia State Bd. of Educ. v. Barnette, 319 U.S. 624, 641 (1943).

12. Id.

13. See generally Nathan Chapman and Michael McConnell, *Agreeing to Disagree: How the Establishment Clause Protects Religious Diversity and Freedom of Conscience* (2023).

14. See Lon L. Fuller, *The Morality of Law* (Yale Univ. Press rev. ed. 1969); Joseph Raz, *The Authority of Law: Essays on Law and Morality* (1979); and John Tasioulas, *The Rule of Law*, in *The Cambridge Companion to the Philosophy of Law* 117 (John Tasioulas ed., 2020).

15. Liberals tend to favor bans on employment discrimination on various grounds, though some people who fit within the liberal tradition do not favor such bans.

16. See Walter J. Blum and Harry Kalven, *The Uneasy Case for Progressive Taxation*, 19 U. Chi. L. Rev. 417 (1952).

17. Mill, supra note 2, at 22.

18. Id. at 101.

19. Liberals disagree about what this phrase means. For example, they favor bans on incestuous marriages, but they may or may not have a problem with bans on marriage between cousins.

20. See, for example, Sarah Conly, *Against Autonomy* (2013).

21. Id.

22. Philip Hamburger, *Is Administrative Law Unlawful?* (2014), can be counted as a liberal book, though some liberals (including this one) vigorously disagree with it.

23. See Richard H. Thaler and Cass R. Sunstein, *Nudge: The Final Edition* (2021).

24. Cass R. Sunstein, *"Come On, Man!" On Errors, Choice, and Hayekian Behavioral Economics*, 7 Behav. Pub. Pol'y 212, 213–217 (2023).

25. See 1 Derek Parfit, *On What Matters* (Samuel Scheffler ed., 2011); and 2 Derek Parfit, *On What Matters* (Samuel Scheffler ed., 2011). Note Parfit's argument that deontology, utilitarianism, and contractarianism converge in important respects.

26. Compare to Robert Frost: "A liberal is a man too broadminded to take his own side in a quarrel." Frost was wrong!

27. See John Rawls, *Political Liberalism: Expanded Edition* 3–22 (Colum. Univ. Press 2005) (1993).

28. See Cass R. Sunstein, *Incompletely Theorized Agreements*, 108 Harv. L. Rev. 1733 (1995).

29. See, for example, Stephen Holmes, *The Anatomy of Antiliberalism* (1993).

30. Daniel Kahneman and Amos Tversky, *On the Reality of Cognitive Illusions*, 103 Psych. Rev. 582, 584 (1996).

31. For a valuable account, see Martha C. Nussbaum, *Perfectionist Liberalism and Political Liberalism*, 39 Phil. & Pub. Affs. 3 (2011). For a helpful overview, see Duncan Bell, *What Is Liberalism?*, 42 Pol. Theory 682 (2014). Rawls, supra note 27, remains defining; its conception of liberalism is often ignored or mischaracterized in contemporary debates. As Nussbaum puts it, "The concept of political liberalism is simply ignored in a large proportion of discussions of welfare and social policy, as are the challenges Rawls poses to thinkers who would base politics on a single comprehensive normative view." Nussbaum, at 6. For an early statement, see Charles Larmore, *Patterns of Moral Complexity* (1987). Also valuable is Stephen Holmes, *Benjamin Constant and the Making of Modern Liberalism* (1984); Stephen Holmes, *Passions and Constraint* (1995). For a clear and broad overview, see Shane D. Courtland, Gerald Gaus, and David Schmidtz, *Liberalism*, Stan. Encyclopedia of Phil. (Spring 2022), https://plato.stanford.edu/entries/liberalism/.

32. Rawls was a political liberal (in the philosophical sense); Mill, like Raz, was a perfectionist liberal.

33. See, for example, Friedrich Hayek, *The Road to Serfdom* (1944).

34. *Socialism* can be defined in many different ways, and some conceptions of socialism are certainly illiberal.

35. See Morton J. Horwitz, *The Rule of Law: An Unqualified Human Good?*, 86 Yale L.J. 561, 566 (1977).

36. See Ronald Dworkin, *Law's Empire* (1985).

37. I put quotation marks around these terms because they seem to me to be insufficiently descriptive of what people actually think. But I later use the terms, and drop the quotation marks, because they nonetheless seem to me to be useful.

38. See Cass R. Sunstein, *Has Liberalism Ruined Everything?*, 19 Contemp. Pol. Theory 175 (2020).

39. Edna Ullmann-Margalit, *Considerateness*, in *Normal Rationality* 226 (Avishai Margalit and Cass R. Sunstein eds., 2017).

40. See Yoram Hazony, *Conservatism: A Rediscovery* (2022).

41. Oliver Wendell Holmes Jr., *Times Change*, Lapham's Q. (1897).

42. See, for example, Friedrich Hayek, *The Origins and Effects of Our Morals: A Problem for Science*, in *The Essence of Hayek* 318 (Chiaki Nishiyama and Kurt Leube eds., 1984).

43. See Ullmann-Margalit, supra note 39.

44. See Mill, supra note 2.

45. See Edna Ullmann-Margalit, *The Emergence of Norms* (1976).

46. See Robert Goodin, *No Smoking* (1989).

47. See id.; Conly, supra note 20.

48. See Jerry Mashaw, *Reasoned Administration and Democratic Legitimacy: How Administrative Law Supports Democratic Government* (2018).

49. John Dewey, *Pragmatic America,* in *America's Public Philosopher: Essays on Social Justice, Economics, Education, and the Future of Democracy* 49, 53 (Eric Thomas Weber ed., 2021).

50. William F. Buckley Jr., *Our Mission Statement*, Nat'l Rev., Nov. 19, 1855, https://www.nationalreview.com/1955/11/our-mission-statement-william-f-buckley-jr/.

CHAPTER 2

1. Buckley, *Our Mission Statement*, Nat'l Rev., Nov. 19, 1855.

2. Id.

3. Id.

4. Id.

5. Paula Span, *Reagan for the Review*, Wash. Post (Dec. 5, 1985), https://www.washingtonpost.com/archive/lifestyle/1985/12/06/reagan-for-the-review/b0a42509-cdcc-4456-8eae-762214a2ede3/.

6. William F. Buckley Jr., *God and Man at Yale* (1951).

7. See William F. Buckley Jr., *Up from Liberalism* (1959).

8. Id. at 201.

9. Id.

10. Id.

11. See Friedrich Hayek, *The Road to Serfdom* (1944).

12. Buckley, supra note 6, at 202.

13. William P. Hustwit, *James J. Kilpatrick: Salesman for Segregation* 33 (2013) (quoting Kilpatrick).

14. Edmund Burke, *Reflections on the Revolution in France* 34, 67 (F. G. Selby ed., 1890) (1790).

15. Id. at 36.

16. Id. at 97.

17. Id. at 107.

18. Id. at 97.

19. See John Stuart Mill, *On Liberty* 101–102 (2nd ed. 1859). See also Elizabeth Anderson, *John Stuart Mill and Experiments in Living*, 102 Ethics 4 (1991). Anderson's essay is deeply illuminating, but it does not explore Mill's relationship with Harriet Taylor, which was, in my view, central to his argument in *On Liberty*.

20. Mill, supra note 19, at 120–121.

21. Again I am bracketing some of the complexities in this idea. See Joseph Raz, *The Morality of Freedom* 412–424 (1988), for valuable discussion, and in particular this suggestion: "Sometimes failing to improve the situation of another is harming him." Id. at 416. For illuminating discussion, see Philip Pettit, *On the People's Terms: A Republican Theory and Model of Democracy* (2013); Philip Pettit, *A Theory of Freedom: From the Psychology to the Politics of Agency* (2001).

22. See West Virginia State Bd. of Educ. v. Barnette, 319 U.S. 624, 641 (1943).

23. Id. at 642.

24. See Meyer v. Nebraska, 262 U.S. 390, 403 (1923); Pierce v. Society of Sisters, 268 US 510, 535 (1925).

25. See Moore v. City of East Cleveland, 431 U.S. 494, 503–06 (1977).

26. See Lawrence v. Texas, 539 U.S. 558, 578 (2003).

27. Suppose, for example, that one of those states takes a distinctive approach to environmental protection or to motor vehicle safety. General propositions do not decide concrete cases (as someone once said), but experiments of living constitutionalism would be strongly inclined to allow such an approach, unless it is plainly inconsistent with federal law.

28. Mill, supra note 19, at 102.

29. See Cass R. Sunstein, *Beyond the Republican Revival*, 97 Yale L.J. 1539 (1988).

30. Abrams v. United States, 250 U.S. 616, 630 (1919).

31. Washington v. Glucksberg, 521 U.S. 702 (1997).

32. Gregory M. Collins, *Cass Sunstein's Limitless Liberalism*, L. & Liberty (Jan. 10, 2024), https://lawliberty.org/cass-sunsteins-limitless-liberalism/.

33. *Is There Life after Liberalism?*, N.Y. Times, Jan. 13, 2018.

34. See Edna Ullmann-Margalit, *The Emergence of Norms* (1977); Edna Ullmann-Margalit, *Normal Rationality* (Avishai Margalit and Cass R. Sunstein eds. 2017).

35. See Edna Ullmann-Margalit, *Considerateness*, in *Normal Rationality*.

36. 3 J. Elliot, *The Debates in the Several State Conventions on the Adoption of the Federal Constitution* 536–537 (1888).

37. This is the basic theme of Cass R. Sunstein, *How to Interpret the Constitution* (2023).

38. My colleague Richard Fallon has explored the idea of reflective equilibrium, and its relationship to constitutional law, to superb effect in Richard Fallon, *Law and Legitimacy in the Supreme Court* (2018). The idea of reflective equilibrium is also used to good effect in Lawrence Solum, *Themes from Fallon on Constitutional Theory*, 18 Geo. J. L. & Pub. Pol'y 287 (2020); Mitchell N. Berman, *Reflective Equilibrium and Constitutional Method: Lessons from John McCain and the Natural-Born Citizenship Clause*, in *The Challenge of Originalism: Theories of Constitutional Interpretation* 246 (Grant Huscroft & Bradley W. Miller eds., 2011).

39. See Rawls, *Theory of Justice* 18 (1971).

40. Id. at 17–18.

41. Id. at 18.

42. Id.

43. Id.

44. Id.

45. Id.

46. Id.

47. Id. at 19.

48. John Rawls, *Political Liberalism* 8 n.8 (1996).

49. Rawls, *Theory of Justice*, supra note 38, at 48.

50. Id.

51. Id.

52. 347 U.S. 483 (1954).

53. 554 US 570 (2008).

54. 395 US 444 (1969).

55. 198 U.S. 45 (1905).

56. 347 U.S. 483 (1954).

57. Obergefell v. Hodges, 576 US 644 (2015).

CHAPTER 3

1. John Stuart Mill, *Socialism* 31 (1879).

2. See Frederick Hayek, 16 *The Collected Works of F. A. Hayek, Hayek on Mill: The Mill-Taylor Friendship and Related Writings* (Sandra J. Peart ed., 2015).

3. Id. at 10.

4. Id.

5. Id. at 298.

6. Id. at 11.

7. Id. at 20.

8. Id. at 21.

9. Id. at 22.

10. Id. at 27.

11. Id. at 33–34.

12. Id. at 37.

13. Id.

14. Id. at 38.

15. Id. at 39.

16. Id. at 48.

17. Id. at 49.

18. Id. at 51.

19. Id. at 55.

20. Id. at 74.

21. Id. at 51.

22. Id. at 93.

23. Id. at 94.

24. Id. at 103.

25. Id. at 152.

26. Id. at 159.

27. Id. at 167.

28. Id. at 167–168.

29. Id. at 168.

30. Id. at 199.

31. Id. at 252.

32. Id. at 253–254.

33. Id. at 256.

34. Id. at 14.

35. Id.

36. The best discussion of this subject remains Edna Ullmann-Margalit, *Invisible-Hand Explanations*, 39 Synthese 263 (1978).

37. Hayek, *Hayek on Mill*, supra note 2, at xlvi; see also Frederick Hayek, *The Fatal Conceit: The Errors of Socialism* (1988).

38. Friedrich Hayek, *The Road to Serfdom* 120 (1944).

39. Hayek, *The Fatal Conceit*, supra note 37, at 136.

40. There continues to be some dispute about whether Mill or Taylor was the true author of *The Enfranchisement of Women*, but the general consensus is in favor of Taylor, and hence that Mill rightly reported when he reprinted the essay and said that it was "hers in a peculiar sense, my share in it being little more than that of an editor and amanuensis." John Stuart Mill, *Dissertations and Discussions* 411 (1859).

41. Harriet Taylor Mill, *The Enfranchisement of Women* 11 (Trübner and Co. ed. 1868) (1851).

42. John Stuart Mill, *On Liberty* 102 (2nd ed. 1859).

43. Id.

44. Hayek, supra note 2, at 312.

45. Id.

46. Id. at 257–258.

CHAPTER 4

1. For superb discussions from which I have learned a great deal, see Lon L. Fuller, *Morality of Law* (Yale Univ. Press rev. ed. 1969); Joseph Raz, *Authority of Law* 213–224 (1979); and John Tasioulas, *The Rule of Law* (2018), available at https://papers.ssrn.com/sol3/papers.cfm?abstract_id=3216796, and in the *Cambridge Companion to the Philosophy of Law* 117–134 (John Tasioulas ed. 2019).

2. Martin Krygier, *Illiberalism and the Rule of Law*, in *Routledge Handbook of Illiberalism* 533, 537 (András Sajó, Renáta Uitz, and Stephen Holmes eds., 2022).

3. A classic discussion can be found in H. L. A. Hart, *The Concept of Law* (1965).

4. Bowen v. Georgetown Univ. Hosp., 488 U.S. 204 (1988).

5. See Henry J. Friendly, *Some Kind of Hearing*, 123 U. Pa. L. Rev. 1267 (1975).

6. Letter from James Madison to Thomas Jefferson (Oct. 24, 1787), in 12 *The Papers of Thomas Jefferson: 7 August 1787 to 31 March 1788* 270, 276 (Julian P. Boyd ed., 1955).

7. Railway Express Agency v. New York, 336 U.S. 106, 116 (1941) (Jackson, J., concurring).

8. Id. at 110.

9. Id. at 112.

10. Id. at 112–113.

11. See also Raz, supra note 1, at 219–223.

12. See generally Friedrich Hayek, *The Constitution of Liberty* (def. ed. 2011).

13. See Friedrich A. Hayek, *The Use of Knowledge in Society*, 4 Am. Econ. Rev. 519 (1945).

14. See Cass R. Sunstein, *The Cost-Benefit Revolution* (2018).

15. Hayek, supra note 12, at 336.

16. Id.

17. Id. at 337.

18. Horwitz, *Rule of Law*, 86 Yale L.J. 566 (1977).

19. See Edna Ullmann-Margalit, *Normal Rationality: Decisions and Social Order* ch. 3 (Avishai Margalit and Cass R. Sunstein eds. 2017); Edna Ullmann-Margalit and Cass R. Sunstein, *Second-Order Decisions*, 110 Ethics 5 (1999).

20. See Stephen Holmes, *Passions and Constraint* (1995).

21. Daniel Kahneman, *Thinking, Fast and Slow* (2010).

22. Consider as well evidence that in the social welfare area, some U.S. courts have insisted on individualized assessments of claimants and thus invalidated regulations that make categorical judgments about when income is actually available to recipients. Perhaps those who issued the regulations were insufficiently attuned to the rigidity and inaccuracy of rules. But perhaps the courts, encountering a particular case that confounded the rules, have been insufficiently attuned to the costs of individuation and hence to the aggregate benefits of rules despite the existence of errors in particular cases. See R. Shep Melnick, *Between the Lines: Interpreting Welfare Rights* (1994).

23. See Daniel Kahneman et al., *Noise* (2021); Daniel Kahneman et al., *Noise: How to Overcome the High, Hidden Cost of Inconsistent Decision Making*, Harv. Bus. Rev. (Oct. 2016), https://hbr.org/2016/10/noise.

24. Dennis v. United States, 341 U.S. 494 (1951).

25. See Frederick Schauer, *Playing by the Rules: A Philosophical Examination of Rule-Based Decision Making in Law and in Life* 136–137 (1991).

26. See Antonin Scalia, *The Rule of Law Is a Law of Rules*, 56 U. Chi. L. Rev. 1175, 1185 (1989).

CHAPTER 5

1. See Alexander Meiklejohn, *Free Speech and Its Relation to Self-Government* (1948).

2. Whitney v. California, 274 U.S. 357, 375 (1927).

3. See Thomas Scanlon, *A Theory of Freedom of Expression*, 1 Phil. & Pub. Affs. 204 (1972).

4. Abrams v. United States, 250 U.S. 616, 630 (1919) (Holmes, J., dissenting).

5. See Seana Shiffrin, *Speech Matters: On Lying, Morality, and the Law* (2014).

6. Id. at 117.

7. John Stuart Mill, *On Liberty* 34 (2nd ed. 1859).

8. DFRLab, *The Criminalization of COVID-19 Clicks and Conspiracies*, Medium, May 13, 2020, https://medium.com/dfrlab/op-ed-the-criminalization-of-covid-19-clicks -and-conspiracies-3af077f5a7e7.

9. Id.

10. Id.

11. Id.

12. *China Vows to Censor Online Covid Chatter over Major Holiday*, Bloomberg, Jan. 18, 2023, https://www.bloomberg.com/news/articles/2023-01-18/china-s-censors-vow -to-wipe-away-gloomy-emotions-over-holiday.

13. 18 U.S.C. § 1621 (2012).

14. 15 U.S.C. § 54 (2012).

15. 18 U.S.C. § 1001.

16. 18 U.S.C. § 912 ("Whoever falsely assumes or pretends to be an officer or employee acting under the authority of the United States or any department, agency or officer thereof, and acts as such . . . shall be fined under this title or imprisoned.").

17. 567 U.S. 709, 723 (2012).

18. Id. at 731–732 (Breyer, J., concurring).

19. Id. at 751–752 (Alito, J., dissenting).

20. Joseph Raz, *Ethics in the Public Domain* 39 (1994).

21. Mill, supra note 7, at 64–67.

22. Id. at 33.

23. Shiffrin, supra note 5, at 140–144.

24. See United States v. Chappell, 691 F.3d 388 (4th Cir. 2012) (ruling that the First Amendment does not ban the "Virginia police impersonation statute, . . . [which] prohibits individuals from falsely assuming or pretending to be a law enforcement officer").

25. Shiffrin, supra note5, at 141.

26. See Timur Kuran, *Public Lies, Private Truths* 78 (1997).

27. For my own treatment of these issues, with a framework for distinguishing what is protected from what is not, see Cass R. Sunstein, *Liars: Falsehoods and Free Speech in an Age of Deception* (2021).

CHAPTER 6

1. Hayek, *Road to Serfdom* 39 (1944).

2. Hayek, *Use of Knowledge,* 4 Am. Econ. Rev. 519 (1945). Superb treatments of Hayek's thought include Peter Boettke, *F.A. Hayek: Economics, Political Economy and Social Philosophy* (2018); and Bruce Caldwell, *Hayek's Challenge: An Intellectual Biography of F.A. Hayek* (2004).

3. Hayek, supra note 2, at 519.

4. Id. at 521.

5. Id. at 527.

6. Id.

7. Hayek, supra note 1, at 17.

8. Id. at 37.

9. Id.

10. See Cass R. Sunstein, *The Cost-Benefit Revolution* (2022).

11. Id. at 38–39.

12. The definition of externalities poses a continuing challenge for liberals. If a polluter harms the health to those who breathe the air in the vicinity, we clearly have an externality. But what if a polluter makes people sad because people do not like pollution?

13. Hayek, *Constitution of Liberty* 71 (def. ed. 2011).

14. Id. at 52.

15. Id.

16. Friedrich Hayek, 15 *The Collected Works of F. A. Hayek: The Market and Other Orders* 386 (Bruce Caldwell ed., 2013).

17. Hayek, supra note 13, at 80.

18. Id. at 81.

19. See Friedrich Hayek, *The Sensory Order* (1952).

20. *Hayek and Behavioral Economics* (Roger Frantz and Robert Leeson eds., 2013) offers many instructive essays on Hayek and his conception of "behavior," but the essays do not claim that behavioral economics, in the form originated and practiced by Robert Shiller, Richard Thaler, David Laibson, George Loewenstein, Matthew Rabin, and others, was anticipated by Hayek's work. Some work that criticizes modern behavioral economics might be loosely described as Hayekian. See, for example, Mario Rizzo and Glen Whitman, *Escaping Paternalism* (2020). But Hayek did not speak to the question of how to handle individual departures from rationality, or argue that apparent departures were no such thing. Some people might want to say, very loosely, that it is in a Hayekian spirit to see various behaviorally suspect choices as an outgrowth of evolved practices and norms so that we should be cautious about interfering with them—but I do not think that it would be good to say that.

21. For one account, see Richard H. Thaler and Cass R. Sunstein, *Nudge: The Final Edition* (2021).

22. Hayek, supra note 16, at 342.

23. John Stuart Mill, *On Liberty* 22 (2nd ed. 1859).

24. Id. at 136–137.

25. Id. at 137.

26. See Sarah Conly, *Against Autonomy* (2013); Ryan Bubb and Richard Pildes, *How Behavioral Economics Trims Its Sails and Why*, 127 Harv. L. Rev. 1593 (2014).

27. See Conly, supra note 26.

28. Hayek, supra note 13, at 489.

29. See Thaler and Sunstein, supra note 21.

30. See Rizzo and Whitman, supra note 20, for some arguments to the latter effect. Very briefly, it is true that an outside observer might not understand the utility function of a chooser. It is also true that what an outsider might take to be present bias, inertia, or limited attention might be nothing of the sort. These points are serious cautionary notes about behaviorally informed interventions. At the same time, departures from rationality are real, and they can create serious trouble, including terrible suffering and unnecessary death. What are we going to do about that?

31. From varying perspectives, but within the same extended family, see, for example, Hunt Allcott et al., *Should We Tax Sugar-Sweetened Beverages? An Overview of Theory and Evidence*, 33 J. Econ. Persps. 202 (2019); B. Douglas Bernheim and Antonio Rangel, *Toward Choice-Theoretic Foundations for Behavioral Welfare Economics*, 97 Am. Econ. Rev. 464 (2007); B. Douglas Bernheim and Antonio Rangel, *Beyond*

Revealed Preference: Choice-Theoretic Foundations for Behavioral Welfare Economics, 124 Q.J. Econ. 51 (2009); B. Douglas Bernheim, *The Good, the Bad, and the Ugly: A Unified Approach to Behavioral Welfare Economics*, 7 J. Benefit-Cost Analysis 12 (2016); B. Douglas Bernheim and Dmitry Taubinsky, *Behavioral Public Economics*, in *Handbook of Behavioral Economics: Foundations and Applications* 1, 381 (B. Douglas Bernheim, Stefano Dellavigna, and David Laibson eds., 2018); Jacob Goldin, *Which Way to Nudge? Uncovering Preferences in the Behavioral Age*, 125 Yale L.J. 226 (2015); and Hunt Allcott and Cass R. Sunstein, *Regulating Internalities*, 34 J. Pol'y Analysis & Mgmt. 698 (2015).

32. See Allcott and Sunstein, supra note 31.

33. Goldin, supra note 31; Jacob Goldin, *Libertarian Quasi-Paternalism*, 82 Missouri L. Rev. 669 (2017). Note, however, that even if consistent choosers are unaffected by frames, they might be affected by some bias, such as present bias or optimistic bias.

34. See Hunt Allcott and Christopher Knittel, *Are Consumers Poorly Informed about Fuel Economy? Evidence from Two Experiments*, 11 Am. Econ. J.: Econ. Pol'y 1 (2019).

35. Cf. Srinath Adusumalli et al., *Effect of Passive Choice and Active Choice Interventions in the Electronic Health Record to Cardiologists on Statin Prescribing: A Cluster Randomized Clinical Trial*, 6 JAMA Cardiology 40 (2021).

36. See Hunt Alcott and Dmitry Taubinsky, *Evaluating Behaviorally Motivated Policy: Experimental Evidence from the Lightbulb Market*, 105 Am. Econ. Rev. 2501 (2015).

37. See Goldin, supra note 33.

38. For a very different perspective, see Robert Sugden, *The Community of Advantage* (2019), which might be taken to offer a Hayekian and thus liberal approach to behavioral economics, one that is far less interested in correction of individual error than the approach defended here. For critical discussion, see Cass R. Sunstein, *Voluntary Agreements*, 29 J. Econ. Methodology 401 (2021). I like to think that my approach is in Mill's spirit.

39. See Felix Ebeling and Sebastian Lotz, *Domestic Uptake of Green Energy Promoted by Opt-out Tariffs*, 5 Nature Climate Change 868 (2015); and Daniel Pichert and Konstantinos V. Katsikopoulos, *Green Defaults: Information Presentation and Pro-environmental Behaviour*, 28 J. Env't Psych. 63 (2008).

40. See Iris Bohnet, *What Works: Gender Equality by Design* (2016); Sendhil Mullainathan and Eldar Shafir, *Scarcity* (2013); George Akerlof and William Dickens, *The Economic Consequences of Cognitive Dissonance*, 72 Am. Econ. Rev. 307 (1982); and Oren Bar-Gill, *Seduction by Contract* (2012).

41. See Akerlof and Dickens, supra note 40.

42. See Allcott and Sunstein, supra note 31.

43. See Allcott et al., supra note 40.

44. Bubb and Pildes, supra note 26, similarly contend that fuel economy regulation might be justified by reference to behavioral considerations, but they focus only on externalities. The conclusion is much easier to justify by reference to internalities, which Bubb and Pildes bracket in their provocative discussion.

45. Valerie Karplus et al., *Should a Vehicle Fuel Economy Standard Be Combined with an Economy-Wide Greenhouse Gas Emission Constraint? Implications for Energy and Climate Policy in the United States*, 36 Energy Econ. 322 (2013).

46. Hayek, supra note 1, at 39.

47. Richard B. Stewart and Jonathan B. Wiener, *Reconstructing Climate Policy: Beyond Kyoto* (2003).

48. See Friedrich Hayek, *Competition as a Discovery Procedure*, in Hayek, *Market and Other Orders*, supra note 16, at 304.

49. For an excellent treatment, see Bruce Ackerman and Richard B. Stewart, *Reforming Environmental Law*, 13 Colum. J. Env't L. 171 (1987).

50. For a defense of carbon taxes, see William Nordhaus, *Climate Change Casino* (2015).

51. See, for example, id.

52. See Cass R. Sunstein and Lucia A. Reisch, *Automatically Green: Behavioral Economics and Environmental Protection*, 38 Harv. Env't L. Rev. 127 (2014).

53. See Karplus et al., supra note 45; Christopher R. Knittel et al., *Diary of a Wimpy Carbon Tax* (MIT Ctr. for Energy & Env't Pol'y Rsch., Working Paper No. 13, 2019), http://ceepr.mit.edu/files/papers/2019-013.pdf; and Lucas W. Davis and Christopher R. Knittel, *Are Fuel Economy Standards Regressive?* (Nat'l Bureau of Econ. Rsch., Working Paper No. 22925, 2016), https://www.nber.org/papers/w22925.

54. Karplus et al., supra note 45, at 322.

55. See Bubb and Pildes, supra note 26.

56. See Richard P. Larrick and Jack B. Soll, *The MPG Illusion*, 320 Science 1593, 1593 (2008).

57. Hayek, supra note 13, at 71.

58. Ted Gayer and W. Kip Viscusi, *Overriding Consumer Preferences with Energy Regulations*, 43 J. Regul. Econ. 248 (2013).

59. See Ralph Hertwig, *When to Consider Boosting: Some Rules for Policy-Makers*, 1 Behav. Pub. Pol'y 143 (2017).

60. See Xavier Gabaix and David Laibson, *Shrouded Attributes, Consumer Myopia, and Information Suppression in Competitive Markets*, 121 Q.J. Econ. 505, 511 (2006).

61. See Xavier Gabaix, *Behavioral Inattention* (Nat'l Bureau of Econ. Rsch., Working Paper No. 24096, 2018), https://www.nber.org/papers/w24096.

62. The hunch is questioned in Allcott and Knittel, supra note 34; James Sallee et al., *Do Consumers Recognize the Value of Fuel Economy? Evidence from Used Car Prices and Gasoline Price Fluctuations*, 135 J. Pub. Econ. 61 (2016); and Meghan Busse et al., *Are Consumers Myopic? Evidence from New and Used Car Purchases*, 103 Am. Econ. Rev. 220 (2013). The hunch is supported in Kenneth Gillingham et al., *Consumer Myopia in Vehicle Purchases* (Nat'l Bureau of Econ. Rsch., Working Paper No. 25845, 2019), https://www.nber.org/papers/w25845. A sharp, balanced discussion can be found in John D. Graham et al., *Co-benefits, Countervailing Risks, and Cost-Benefit Analysis* (2019) (on file at https://www.hsph.harvard.edu/wp-content/uploads/sites/1273/2019/09/Graham-Wiener-Robinson-2019.pdf), with what seems to me a prudent conclusion: "It seems that agency analysts should adopt a middle-ground position between full consumer valuation of fuel economy and no consumer valuation of fuel economy, and perform sensitivity analyses with different partial degrees of consumer valuation." Id. at 20.

63. For suggestive evidence, see Richard Newell and Juha Siikamaki, *Individual Time Preferences and Energy Efficiency* (Nat'l Bureau of Econ. Rsch., Working Paper No. 20969, 2015), https://www.nber.org/papers/w20969. Note that the miles-per-gallon measure is hardly hidden, and there is nothing quite as salient for energy efficiency.

64. See *Light-Duty Vehicle Greenhouse Gas Emission Standards and Corporate Average Fuel Economy Standards; Final Rule*, Part II, 75 Fed. Reg. 25,324, 25,510–11 (May 7, 2010).

65. Hayek, Constitution of Liberty, supra note 13, at 50.

66. For valuable, inconclusive discussions, see Hunt Allcott, *Paternalism and Energy Efficiency: An Overview*, 8 Ann. Rev. Econ. 145 (2016); and Hunt Allcott and Michael Greenstone, *Is There an Energy Efficiency Gap?*, 26 J. Econ. Persps. 3 (2012).

67. See Sallee et al., supra note 62; and Busse et al., supra note 62.

68. See Allcott and Knittel, supra note 34.

69. See Gillingham et al., supra note 62.

70. Id.

71. Denvil Duncan et al., *Most Consumers Don't Buy Hybrids: Is Rational Choice a Sufficient Explanation?*, 10 J. Benefit-Cost Analysis 1 (2019).

72. See Graham et al., supra note 62, at 19.

73. See Gayer and Viscusi, supra note 58.

74. See Conly, supra note 26.

75. See id.; and Gayer and Viscusi, supra note 58.

76. See, for example, Natasha Sarin, *Making Consumer Finance Work*, 119 Colum. L. Rev. 1519 (2019).

CHAPTER 7

1. Baron de Montesquieu, *The Spirit of the Laws* 25 (Hafner Press 1949) (1748).

2. Franklin Delano Roosevelt, Eleventh Annual Message to Congress (Jan. 11, 1944), in *The Essential Franklin Delano Roosevelt* 290, 295 (John Gabriel Hunt ed., 1995).

3. Lester Ward, *Plutocracy and Paternalism* (1895), quoted in Sidney Fine, *Laissez Faire and the General Welfare State* 262 (1919).

4. Franklin Delano Roosevelt, Campaign Address on Progressive Government at the Commonwealth Club in San Francisco, California (Sept. 23, 1932) (transcript available at the American Presidency Project).

5. Franklin Delano Roosevelt, Annual Message to Congress on the State of the Union (Jan. 6, 1941) (transcript available at the American Presidency Project).

6. Id.

7. Id.

8. Franklin Delano Roosevelt, State of the Union Message to Congress (Jan. 11, 1944) (transcript available at the American Presidency Project).

9. In specialized circles, of course, the Second Bill has been discussed, though even here it receives brief attention. Consider, for example, the illuminating but brisk treatment in David M. Kennedy, *Freedom from Fear: The American People in Depression and War, 1929–1945* 784–786 (1999).

10. Roosevelt, Campaign Address, supra note 4.

11. Franklin Delano Roosevelt, Address to Congress Requesting a Declaration of War with Japan (Dec. 8, 1941) (transcript available at the American Presidency Project).

12. Doris Kearns Goodwin, *No Ordinary Time: Franklin and Eleanor Roosevelt: The Home Front in World War II* 313 (1994).

13. Roosevelt, 1944 State of the Union, supra note 8.

14. Id.

15. Id.

16. Id.

17. Id.

18. Id.

19. Id.

20. Id.

21. Id.

22. Id.

23. Id.

24. Id.

25. Id.

26. Id.

27. Here Roosevelt was quoting, not for the first time, from a British judge: "Necessitous men," wrote the Lord Chancellor in Vernon v. Bethell, 2 Eden 113 (1762), "are not, truly speaking, free men; but, to answer a present emergency, will submit to any terms that the crafty may impose on them."

28. Roosevelt, 1944 State of the Union, supra note 8.

29. Id.

30. Id.

31. Id.

32. Id.

33. Id.

34. Id.

35. Id.

36. Id.

37. Id.

38. Goodwin, supra note 12, at 481–482.

39. Time, Jan. 24, 1944, at 12–14.

40. See Kennedy, supra note 9, at 786–787.

41. Id. at 787.

42. Franklin Delano Roosevelt, Speech Before the 1932 Democratic National Convention (July 2, 1932), in *Essential Franklin Delano Roosevelt*, supra note 2, at 17.

43. Id. at 26.

44. Id. at 27.

45. Id.

46. Id. at 29.

47. See Samuel I. Rosenman, *Working with Roosevelt* 71 (1952).

48. Franklin Delano Roosevelt, 2 *The Public Papers and Addresses of Franklin D. Roosevelt: The Year of Crisis, 1933* 5 (1938).

49. Goodwin, supra note 12, at 485.

50. Jeremy Bentham, *Principles of the Civil Code*, in *Theory of Legislation* 88, 113 (Richard Hildreth trans., 2nd ed. 1871).

51. See Robert Hale, *Coercion and Distribution in a Supposedly Non-coercive State*, 38 Pol. Sci. Q. 470 (1923); and Morris R. Cohen, *Property and Sovereignty*, 13 Cornell L.Q. 8 (1927).

52. Robert L. Hale, *Current Political and Economic Review*, 8 Am. Bar Assoc. J. 638, 638 (1922).

53. Int'l News Serv. v. Assoc. Press, 248 U.S. 215, 246 (1918) (Holmes, J., concurring).

54. Robert Hale, *Rate Making and the Revision of the Property Concept*, 22 Colum. L. Rev. 209, 214 (1922) (emphasis added).

55. Warren J. Samuels, *The Economy as a System of Power and Its Legal Bases: The Legal Economics of Robert Lee Hale*, 27 U. Mia. L. Rev. 261, 326 (1973).

56. Hale, supra note 52, at 538.

57. Id. at 539. A similar point was made by Gerald Henderson in 1920; see Gerald C. Henderson, *Railway Valuation and the Courts*, 33 Harv. L. Rev. 902 (1920). Henderson describes a situation in which a company lawyer argues to a ratesetting commission that the company should "be allowed always a certain percentage on the value of the property. If value goes up, rates should go on proportionately." Henderson, supra, at 917. But an economist, Henderson notes, could respond "that the only accepted and sensible meaning of the word 'value' is 'value in exchange.'" Henderson, supra. And "value in exchange" is in turn a function of "what we allow you gentlemen to charge the public. If we reduce your rates, your value goes down. . . . Obviously we cannot measure rates by value, if value is itself a function of rates" (some internal quotations omitted). Henderson, supra. In this way, Henderson made the point—all over the legal culture in the period—that property rights and economic values were a creature of regulatory decisions.

58. Hale, supra note 54, at 214.

59. Note, *The Peppercorn Theory of Consideration and the Doctrine of Fair Exchange in Contract Law*, 35 Colum. L. Rev. 1090, 1091–1092 (1935) (emphasis added).

60. Ward, supra note 3, at 262. An excellent discussion of this period is Barbara Fried, *Robert Hale and Progressive Law and Economics* (1993).

61. Hayek, *Road to Serfdom* 38 (1944).

62. Id.

63. Id. at 39.

64. Kennedy, supra note 9, at 116.

65. Roosevelt, Speech Before the 1932 Democratic National Convention, supra note 42, at 27.

66. Id.

67. Roosevelt, Campaign Address on Progressive Government, supra note 4.

68. Franklin Delano Roosevelt, Letter from the President's Committee on Economic Security Transmitted to Congress with the Foregoing Message (Jan. 17, 1935) (available at the American Presidency Project). See also Cohen, supra note 51, which makes similar points.

69. Franklin Delano Roosevelt, Campaign Address on a Program for Unemployment and Long-Range Planning at Boston, Massachusetts (Oct. 31, 1932) (transcript available at the American Presidency Project).

70. 29 U.S.C. § 102 (emphasis added).

71. Amartya Sen, *Poverty and Famines* (1981), is a striking contemporary illustration of similar ideas, demonstrating that famines are a result not of a decrease in the supply of food, but of social choices—prominent among them legal ones, deciding who is entitled to what. See especially id. at 166: "The law stands between food availability and food entitlement. Starvation deaths can reflect legality with a vengeance." This claim can be seen as a special case of the New Deal understanding of "laissez-faire." See also Jean Dreze and Amartya Sen, *Hunger and Public Action* (1991) (demonstrating that both famines and entrenched hunger are artifacts of identifiable social policies, rather than a consequence of "nature").

72. Fried, supra note 60, at 89 (quoting a letter from Hale to Elliot Cheatham).

73. Cohen, supra note 51, at 14.

74. 2 *The Public Papers and Addresses of Franklin D. Roosevelt* 72 (1938). See also Rex Tugwell, *The Struggle for Democracy* (1935), which emphasizes experimentation on nearly every page.

75. 1 *Public Papers and Addresses of Franklin D. Roosevelt* 778 (1938).

76. The Federalist No. 70 (Alexander Hamilton).

77. 1 *Annals of Cong.* 733–745 (Joseph Gales ed., 1789).

78. See Gordon Wood, *The Radicalism of the American Revolution* 272 (1993).

79. See Franklin Delano Roosevelt, *Whither Bound?* (1926).

80. Id. at 4.

81. Id. at 5.

82. Id. at 19.

83. Id. at 22.

84. Id. at 25.

85. Id. at 24.

86. Id. at 24–25.

87. Id. at 27.

88. Id.

89. Id. at 27–28.

90. Id. at 28.

91. Id. at 30.

92. Id. at 31.

93. Id. at 32.

94. Id.

95. Roosevelt, Speech Before the 1932 Democratic National Convention, supra note 42, at 27.

96. Roosevelt, Campaign Address on Progressive Government, supra note 4.

CHAPTER 8

1. See Howard Fishman, *To Anyone Who Ever Asks* (2023).

2. Id. at 329.

3. Id.

4. Id. at 328.

5. Id. at 26.

6. Id. at 485.

7. Id. at 445.

8. Matthew J. Salganik et al., *Experimental Study of Inequality and Unpredictability in an Artificial Cultural Market*, 311 Science 854 (2006).

9. Mark Olsen, *Oscars 2013: "Searching for Sugar Man" Wins Best Documentary*, L.A. Times, Feb. 24, 2013, https://www.latimes.com/entertainment/envelope/la-xpm-2013 -feb-24-la-et-mn-oscars-2013-best-documentary-20130220-story.html.

10. Bob Simon, *Rodriguez: The Rock Icon Who Didn't Know It*, CBS News, Oct. 8, 2012, https://www.cbsnews.com/news/rodriguez-the-rock-icon-who-didnt-know-it/.

11. Alex Bell et al., *Who Becomes an Inventor in America? The Importance of Exposure to Innovation*, 134 Q.J. Econ. 647 (2019).

12. Mill, *Subjection of Women* 10 (1869).

13. Id. at 29–30.

14. See Jill Lepore, *Book of Ages: The Life and Opinions of Jane Franklin* 218 (2014).

15. Id.

16. See id. at xi. For relevant discussion of freedom, see Philip Pettit, *The Instability of Freedom as Noninterference: The Case of Isaiah Berlin*, 121 Ethics 693 (2011).

EPILOGUE

1. Franklin D. Roosevelt, Address at the Annual Dinner of White House Correspondents' Association (1941), available at https://www.presidency.ucsb.edu/documents/address-the-annual-dinner-white-house-correspondents-association.

2. Mill, *On Liberty* 33 (2nd ed. 1859).

3. Mill, *Subjection of Women* 1 (1869).

4. Benjamin Constant, *Principles of Politics Applicable to All Governments* 103 (Dennis O'Keefe trans., Liberty Fund ed. 2003) (1815).

5. Rawls, *Theory of Justice* 587 (1971).

INDEX